Modern Critical Interpretations
Christopher Marlowe's
Doctor Faustus

Modern Critical Interpretations

These and other titles in preparation

Modern Critical Interpretations

Christopher Marlowe's

Doctor Faustus

Edited and with an introduction by
Harold Bloom
Sterling Professor of the Humanities
Yale University

Chelsea House Publishers ◊ *1988*

NEW YORK ◊ NEW HAVEN ◊ PHILADELPHIA

90-3118

© 1988 by Chelsea House Publishers, a division
of Chelsea House Educational Communications, Inc.

Introduction © 1988 by Harold Bloom

Printed and bound in the United States of America

10 9 8 7 6 5 4 3 2 1

∞ The paper used in this publication meets the minimum
requirements of the American National Standard for Permanence
of Paper for Printed Library Materials, Z39.48–1984.

Library of Congress Cataloging-in-Publication Data
Christopher Marlowe's Doctor Faustus / edited and with an
introduction by Harold Bloom.
    p.   cm.—(Modern critical interpretations)
  Bibliography: p.
  Includes index.
  Summary: A collection of seven critical essays on Marlowe's
drama, arranged in chronological order of their original
publication.
  ISBN 0–87754–915–X (alk. paper) : $19.95
  1. Marlowe, Christopher, 1564–1593. Doctor Faustus.
2. Faust, d. ca. 1540, in fiction, drama, poetry,
etc. [1. Marlowe, Christopher, 1564–1593. Doctor
Faustus.   2. Faust, d. ca. 1540, in fiction, drama, poetry,
etc. 3. English literature—History and criticism.] I. Bloom,
Harold.   II. Series.
PR2664.C48   1988
822'.3—dc19   87–22190
                                              CIP
                                              AC

Contents

Editor's Note

This book gathers together a representative selection of the best modern critical interpretations of Christopher Marlowe's drama *Doctor Faustus*. The critical essays are reprinted here in the chronological order of their original publication. I am grateful to John Rogers and Susan Laity for their aid in editing this volume.

My introduction, after deprecating the modern scholarly fashion of baptizing Marlowe's rather heterodox imagination, moves from a consideration of Barabas in *The Jew of Malta* to a related examination of Mephostophilis as the true hero–villain of *Doctor Faustus*.

The chronological sequence of criticism begins with G. K. Hunter, who believes Marlowe to be the sole author of the play, which he feels follows the typical Elizabethan five-act structure and is thematically integrated. In considering Faustus's sin, Wilbur Sanders, rather differently, sees the play as alternating moments of intense power and of vapid bathos (which I suspect we owe to Rowley, not to the fierce Marlowe).

In Edward A. Snow's acute reading, the drama is what I would call High Romantic, reminding us that Marlowe was a crucial precursor of the English Romantic poets. Like Blake and Shelley, Marlowe is concerned with the aims and the limits of human desire. Barbara Howard Traister, following in the wake of Sanders, also discusses how Marlowe deliberately debases Faustus's status and performance as a magician, so that Faustus achieves mastery only in self-delusion. *will an audience see this?*

The relation of Faustus's language to both his power and powerlessness is the subject of Johannes H. Birringer, who judges that a kind of power is achieved by the Marlovian "rhetoric of aspiration." Jonathan Dollimore analyzes the contention in *Doctor Faustus* between orthodoxy and heterodoxy, and sees Marlowe as accomplishing a subversion of Protestant theology through the drama of transgression. In the concluding essay, Christopher Ricks finds the great plague of 1592–94 to be the subtext informing Marlowe's look at Hell on earth.

New critics → N Hist

Introduction

Like Shakespeare, born only a few months after him, Marlowe began as
an Ovidian poet. Killed at twenty-nine, in what may have been a mere
tavern brawl or possibly a political intrigue (fitter end for a double agent),
Marlowe had the unhappy poetic fate of being swallowed up by Shakespeare's unprecedented powers of dramatic representation. We read Marlowe now as Shakespeare's precursor, remembering that Shakespeare also
began as a poet of Ovidian eros. Read against Shakespeare, Marlowe all
but vanishes. Nor can anyone prophesy usefully how Marlowe might
have developed if he had lived another quarter century. There seems little
enough development between *Tamburlaine* (1587) and *Doctor Faustus*
(1593), and perhaps Marlowe was incapable of that process we name by
the critical trope of "poetic development," which seems to imply a kind
of turning about or even a wrapping up.

There has been a fashion in modern scholarly criticism to baptize
Marlowe's imagination, so that a writer of tragic caricatures has been
converted into an orthodox moralist. The vanity of scholarship has few
more curious monuments than this Christianized Marlowe. What the
common reader finds in Marlowe is precisely what his contemporaries
found: impiety, audacity, worship of power, ambiguous sexuality, occult
aspirations, defiance of moral order, and above all else a sheer exaltation
of the possibilities of rhetoric, of the persuasive force of heroic poetry.
The subtlest statement of the scholar's case is made by Frank Kermode:

> Thus Marlowe displays his heroes reacting to most of the
> temptations that Satan can contrive; and the culminating
> temptation . . . is the scholar's temptation, forbidden knowl-
> edge. . . . [Marlowe's] heroes do not resist the temptations,
> and he provides us, not with a negative proof of virtue and

obedience to divine law, but with positive examples of what happens in their absence. Thus, whatever his intentions may have been, and however much he flouted conventions, Marlowe's themes are finally reducible to the powerful formulae of contemporary religion and morality.

"Finally reducible" is the crucial phrase here; is final reduction the aim of reading or of play-going? As for "Marlowe's themes," they count surely rather less than Marlowe's rhetoric does, and, like most themes or topics, indubitably do ensue ultimately from religion and morality. But Marlowe is not Spenser or Milton and there is one originality he possesses that is not subsumed by Shakespeare. Call that originality by the name of Barabas, Marlowe's grandest character, who dominates what is certainly Marlowe's most vital and original play, *The Jew of Malta.* Barabas defies reduction, and his gusto represents Marlowe's severest defiance of all moral and religious convention.

II

Barabas (or Barabbas, as in the Gospels) means "son of the Father" and so "son of God" and may have begun as an alternate name for Jesus. As the anti-Jewish tenor of the Gospels intensified from Mark to John, Barabbas declined from a patriotic insurrectionist to a thief, and as either was preferred by "the Jews" to Jesus. This is a quite Marlovian irony that the scholar Hyam Maccoby puts forward, and Marlowe might have rejoiced at the notion that Jesus and Barabbas were historically the same person. One Richard Baines, a police informer, insisted that Marlowe said of Jesus: "If the Jews among whom he was born did crucify him they best knew him and whence he came." The playwright Thomas Kyd, arrested after his friend Marlowe's death, testified that the author of *The Jew of Malta* tended to "jest at the divine Scriptures, gibe at prayers, and strive in argument to frustrate and confute what hath been spoke or writ by prophets and such holy men." Are we to credit Baines and Kyd, or Kermode and a bevy of less subtle scholars?

Marlowe, who was as sublimely disreputable as Rimbaud or Hart Crane, is more of their visionary company than he is at home with T. S. Eliot or with academic moralists. *The Jew of Malta* contrasts sharply with *The Merchant of Venice,* which may have been composed so as to overgo it on the stage. It cannot be too much emphasized that Marlowe's Barabas is a savage original, while Shakespeare's Shylock, despite his supposed humanization, is essentially the timeless anti-Semitic stock figure, devil and usurer, of Christian tradition. Stating it more plainly, Shakespeare indeed is as anti-Semitic as the Gospels or T. S. Eliot, whereas Marlowe employs his Barabas as a truer surrogate for himself than are Tamburlaine, Edward II, and Dr. Faustus. Barabas is Marlowe the satirist:

> It's no sin to deceive a Christian;
> For they themselves hold it a principle,
> Faith is not to be held with heretics;
> But all are heretics that are not Jews;
> This follows well.
>
> (2.3.313–17)

And so indeed it does. The art of Barabas is to better Christian instruction, unlike that of Shylock, who has persistence but who lacks art. Shylock is obsessive-compulsive; Barabas delights because he is a free man, or, if you would prefer, a free fiend, at once a monstrous caricature and a superb image of Marlowe's sly revenge upon society. What Hazlitt gave us as a marvelous critical concept, gusto, is superbly manifested by Barabas, but not by poor Shylock. "Gusto in art is power or passion defining any object." Hazlitt accurately placed Shakespeare first among writers in this quality:

> The infinite quantity of dramatic invention in Shakespeare takes from his gusto. The power he delights to show is not intense, but discursive. He never insists on anything he might, except a quibble.

But Shylock is the one great exception in Shakespeare and, surprisingly, lacks invention. Marlowe's superior gusto, in just this one instance, emerges as we contrast two crucial speeches. Barabas is outrageous, a parody of the stage-Jew, and Shylock speaks with something like Shakespeare's full resources, so that the power of language is overwhelmingly Shakespeare's, and yet Barabas becomes an original representation, while Shylock becomes even more the nightmare bogey of Christian superstition and hatred:

> SALERIO: Why, I am sure if he forfeit thou wilt not take his
> flesh. What's that good for?
> SHYLOCK: To bait fish withal—if it will feed nothing else, it
> will feed my revenge. He hath disgrac'd me, and
> hind'red me half a million, laugh'd at my losses,

> mock'd at my gains, scorn'd my nation, thwarted my
> bargains, cool'd my friends, heated mine enemies; and
> what's his reason? I am a Jew. Hath not a Jew eyes?
> Hath not a Jew hands, organs, dimensions, senses,
> affections, passions; fed with the same food, hurt with
> the same weapons, subject to the same diseases, heal'd
> by the same means, warm'd and cool'd by the same
> winter and summer, as a Christian is? If you prick us,
> do we not bleed? If you tickle us, do we not laugh? If
> you poison us, do we not die? And if you wrong us,
> shall we not revenge? If we are like you in the rest, we
> will resemble you in that. If a Jew wrong a Christian,
> what is his humility? Revenge. If a Christian wrong a
> Jew, what should his sufferance be by Christian
> example? Why, revenge. The villainy you teach me, I
> will execute, and it shall go hard but I will better the
> instruction.
>
> (3.1.51–73)

"If you prick us, do we not bleed? If you tickle us, do we not laugh?" Shylock himself is not changed by listening to these, his own words, and neither are the audience's prejudices changed one jot. No one in that audience had seen a Jew, nor had Shakespeare, unless they or he had watched the execution of the unfortunate Dr. Lopez, the Queen's physician, condemned on a false charge of poisoning, or had glimpsed one of the handful of other converts resident in London. Shylock is rendered more frightening by the startling reminders that this dangerous usurer is flesh and blood, a man as well as a devil. Jews after all, Shakespeare's language forcefully teaches his audience, are not merely mythological murderers of Christ and of his beloved children, but literal seekers after the flesh of the good and gentle Antonio.

Can we imagine Barabas saying: "If you prick us, do we not bleed? If you tickle us, do we not laugh?" Or can we imagine Shylock intoning this wonderful and parodistic outburst of the exuberant Barabas?

> As for myself, I walk abroad a-nights,
> And kill sick people groaning under walls:
> Sometimes I go about and poison wells;
> And now and then, to cherish Christian thieves,
> I am content to lose some of my crowns;
> That I may, walking in my gallery,

See 'em go pinioned along by my door.
Being young I studied physic, and began
To practise first upon the Italian;
There I enriched the priests with burials,
And always kept the sexton's arms in ure
With digging graves and ringing dead men's knells:
And after that was I an engineer,
And in the wars 'twixt France and Germany,
Under pretence of helping Charles the Fifth,
Slew friend and enemy with my stratagems.
Then after that was I an usurer,
And with extorting, cozening, forfeiting,
And tricks belonging unto brokery,
I filled the jails with bankrouts in a year,
And with young orphans planted hospitals,
And every moon made some or other mad,
And now and then one hang himself for grief,
Pinning upon his breast a long great scroll
How I with interest tormented him.
But mark how I am blest for plaguing them,
I have as much coin as will buy the town.
But tell me now, how hast thou spent thy time?
(2.3.178–205)

This would do admirably in a Gilbert and Sullivan opera, had the anti-Semitic Gilbert (see *The Bab Ballads*) been willing to mock his own prejudices. We do not know how the more sophisticated among Marlowe's audience received this, but properly delivered it has the tang and bite of great satire. A more fascinating surmise is: How did Shakespeare receive this? And how did he react to Barabas in what we can call the mode of Hemingway, sparring with his holy friars?

2 FRIAR: Barabas, thou hast—
1 FRIAR: Ay, that thou hast—
BARABAS: True, I have money, what though I have?
2 FRIAR: Thou art a—
1 FRIAR: Ay, that thou art, a—
BARABAS: What needs all this? I know I am a Jew.
2 FRIAR: Thy daughter—
1 FRIAR: Ay, thy daughter—
BARABAS: Oh speak not of her, then I die with grief.

> 2 FRIAR: Remember that—
> 1 FRIAR: Ay, remember that—
> BARABAS: I must needs say that I have been a great usurer.
> 2 FRIAR: Thou hast committed—
> BARABAS: Fornication? but that was in another country: and
>   besides, the wench is dead.
>
> (4.1.28–42)

We can say that Shakespeare refused the hint. Shylock's grim repetitions ("I will have my bond") come out of a different universe, the crimes of Christendom that Shakespeare had no thought of rejecting. This is hardly to say that Marlowe was in any sense humane. *The Jew of Malta* is bloody farce, more than worthy of Jarry or Artaud. Barabas emerges from the world of Thomas Nashe and Thomas Kyd, Marlowe's half-world of espionage and betrayal, of extravagant wit and antithetical lusts, which was the experiential scene that must have taught Shakespeare to go and live otherwise, and write otherwise as well.

III

The Australian poet Alex Hope, in a remarkable essay upon Marlowe, ascribes to *Tamburlaine* "a thorough-going morality of power, aesthetics of power and logic of power." Hope is clearly right about *Tamburlaine*. I would go further and suggest that there is no other morality, aesthetics, or logic anywhere in Marlowe's writings. Where Hope usefully quotes Hazlitt on the congruence between the language of power and the language of poetry, I would cite also the great American theoretician of power and poetry, the Emerson of *The Conduct of Life*:

> A belief in causality, or strict connection between every trifle and the principle of being, and, in consequence, belief in compensation, or, that nothing is got for nothing,—characterizes all valuable minds, and must control every effort that is made by an industrious one. The most valiant men are the best believers in the tension of the laws. . . .
>
> All power is of one kind, a sharing of the nature of the world. The mind that is parallel with the laws of nature will be in the current of events, and strong with their strength.

Like Marlowe, Hazlitt and Emerson are agonists who understand that there are no accidents. In Marlowe, the implicit metaphysics of this understanding are Epicurean-Lucretian. Barabas and Tamburlaine seek their own freedom, and ultimately fail, but only because they touch the ultimate limits at the flaming ramparts of the world. Edward II and Dr. Faustus fail, but they are weak and their fate does not grieve Marlowe. Indeed, the aesthetic satisfaction Marlowe hints at is not free from a sadistic pleasure the poet and his audience share at observing the dreadful ends of Edward and Faustus. Marlowe's heroes, Tamburlaine and Barabas, die defiantly, with Tamburlaine still naming himself "the scourge of God," and Barabas, boiling in a cauldron, nevertheless cursing his enemies with his customary vehemence:

> And villains, know you cannot help me now.
> Then Barabas breathe forth thy latest fate,
> And in the fury of thy torments, strive
> To end thy life with resolution:
> Know, Governor, 'twas I that slew thy son;
> I framed the challenge that did make them meet:
> Know, Calymath, I aimed thy overthrow,
> And had I but escaped this stratagem,
> I would have brought confusion on you all,
> Damned Christian dogs, and Turkish infidels;
> But now begins the extremity of heat
> To pinch me with intolerable pangs:
> Die life, fly soul, tongue curse thy fill and die.
>   (5.5.79–91)

Shylock, alas, ends wholly broken, "content" to become a Christian, a resolution that is surely the most unsatisfactory in all of Shakespeare. I cannot envision the late Groucho Marx playing Shylock, but I sometimes read through *The Jew of Malta* mentally casting Groucho as Barabas. T. S. Eliot, whose admiration for *The Jew of Malta* was strong, was also a fan of the sublime Groucho. I rejoice, for once, to share two of Eliot's enthusiasms and enjoy the thought that he too might have wished to see Groucho play Barabas.

IV

Though it seems to me less impressive than *The Jew of Malta* and the first part of *Tamburlaine*, *Doctor Faustus* is now regarded by most critics as Marlowe's greatest play. I have seen several performances of *Doctor Faustus* and of *Edward II*, but only one of *Tamburlaine* (a superb enactment by Anthony Quayle) and regret deeply that I have not yet seen

The Jew of Malta on stage. Marlowe had a collaborator (perhaps two) in *Doctor Faustus,* and we do not seem to have an authentic text of the play. Many of the comic scenes are scarcely readable, and no other Elizabethan play mixes superb and dreadful writing to the extent that this one does.

Marlowe, whose learning was curious and extensive, presumably knew that Faustus (Latin for "the favored one") was the cognomen taken by Simon Magus, founder of the Gnostic heresy, when he went to Rome. *Doctor Faustus* is a Hermetic drama in its range and implications, but it has few Gnostic overtones. It scarcely matters whether its overt theology is Catholic, Lutheran, or Calvinist, since the theology is there as a good, boisterous mythology that the hyperbolist Marlowe is happy to exploit. As many critics have recognized, Marlowe maintains his distance from Faustus and expresses himself fairly directly through the splendidly bitter Mephostophilis, who walks about in the likeness of a friar and who suffers a profound nostalgia for the loss of heaven. Marlowe is not representing himself in or as Mephostophilis and yet clearly Mephostophilis, not Faustus, is the play's intellectual, its advanced, or modern, thinker. He cannot exactly be called disinterested and yet he is remarkably detached, while carefully always knowing both his limits and his allegiances. Though a loyal follower of Lucifer, his rhetoric indicates a personal and poignant distance from his own camp and conveys a more formidable pathos than Faustus himself will evoke until his final speech. The opening dialogue between Faustus and his personal devil (as it were) provides a remarkable dramatic contrast between the two, a contrast in which we find we prefer Mephostophilis to the human magus who thinks he has summoned this spirit:

> MEPHOSTOPHILIS: I am a servant to great Lucifer,
>   And may not follow thee without his leave;
>   No more than he commands must we perform.
> FAUSTUS: Did not he charge thee to appear to me?
> MEPHOSTOPHILIS: No, I came now hither of mine own
>   accord.
> FAUSTUS: Did not my conjuring speeches raise thee? Speak.
> MEPHOSTOPHILIS: That was the cause, but yet *per accidens;*
>   For when we hear one rack the name of God,
>   Abjure the scriptures and his saviour Christ,
>   We fly in hope to get his glorious soul;
>   Nor will we come unless he use such means
>   Whereby he is in danger to be damned.

Therefore the shortest cut for conjuring
Is stoutly to abjure the Trinity
And pray devoutly to the prince of hell.
FAUSTUS: So Faustus hath already done, and holds this
    principle:
There is no chief but only Belzebub,
To whom Faustus doth dedicate himself.
This word "damnation" terrifies not him,
For he confounds hell in Elysium.
His ghost be with the old philosophers.
But leaving these vain trifles of men's souls,
Tell me, what is that Lucifer, thy lord?
MEPHOSTOPHILIS: Arch-regent and commander of all spirits.
FAUSTUS: Was not that Lucifer an angel once?
MEPHOSTOPHILIS: Yes Faustus, and most dearly loved of God.
FAUSTUS: How come it then that he is prince of devils?
MEPHOSTOPHILIS: O, by aspiring pride and insolence,
    For which God threw him from the face of heaven.
FAUSTUS: And what are you that live with Lucifer?
MEPHOSTOPHILIS: Unhappy spirits that fell with Lucifer,
    Conspired against our God with Lucifer,
    And are for ever damned with Lucifer.
FAUSTUS: Where are you damned?
MEPHOSTOPHILIS: In hell.
FAUSTUS: How comes it then that thou art out of hell?
MEPHOSTOPHILIS: Why, this is hell, nor am I out of it.
    Think'st thou that I who saw the face of God
    And tasted the eternal joys of heaven,
    Am not tormented with ten thousand hells
    In being deprived of everlasting bliss?
    O Faustus, leave these frivolous demands,
    Which strikes a terror to my fainting soul.

(3.40–82)

Lucifer would not be pleased by the language of his loyal but elaborately wistful follower, we must suspect. The hints that Milton took from Marlowe are plain enough, but even the sublimity of the Miltonic Satan of the early books of *Paradise Lost* does not allow for anything quite like the epigrammatic snap of the justly famous "Why, this is hell, nor am I out of it," the most Gnostic statement in the drama. Harry Levin rather strangely compared Mephostophilis to Dostoevsky's Porfiry, the examining magistrate in *Crime and Punishment*. But Porfiry is a good man; Mephostophilis, I venture, is Marlowe's version of the Accuser, the Satan who appears at the opening of the Book of Job. Blake, in a Gnostic insight, called the Accuser the God of this world. Mephostophilis has no such pretensions and is closer to the biblical Book of Job's Accuser because he functions as what Saul Bellow rather nastily calls a Reality Instructor. Mephostophilis has uncanny insight into Faustus, indeed he seems to be the Daemon or Genius of Faustus, perhaps the spiritual form that Faustus will take on in Hell.

Mephostophilis has a horror of marriage, not merely because it is a sacrament but because this "ceremonial toy" might threaten his curious intimacy with Faustus. This aversion to connubial bliss is mild compared to the exalted view of man held by this surprising spirit, who seems both more of a Hermeticist and more of a Humanist than either Marlowe or Faustus:

> FAUSTUS: When I behold the heavens then I repent,
> And curse thee, wicked Mephostophilis,
> Because thou hast deprived me of those joys.
> MEPHOSTOPHILIS: 'Twas thine own seeking, Faustus, thank thyself.
> But think'st thou heaven is such a glorious thing?
> I tell thee, Faustus, it is not half so fair
> As thou or any man that breathes on earth.
> FAUSTUS: How prov'st thou that?
> MEPHOSTOPHILIS: 'Twas made for man; then he's more excellent.
> FAUSTUS: If heaven was made for man, 'twas made for me.
> I will renounce this magic and repent.
>
> (6.1–11)

Mephostophilis evidently desires Faustus, at least aesthetically, and we remember his initial insistence that he first came to Faustus not because he was conjured, but of his own accord. Forbidden by Lucifer to love the creator, Mephostophilis loves the creature and refuses to discuss origins:

> FAUSTUS: Well, I am answered. Now tell me, who made the world?
> MEPHOSTOPHILIS: I will not.
> FAUSTUS: Sweet Mephostophilis, tell me.

MEPHOSTOPHILIS: Move me not, Faustus.
FAUSTUS: Villain, have not I bound thee to tell me anything?
MEPHOSTOPHILIS: Ay, that is not against our kingdom:
 This is. Thou art damned, think thou of hell.
FAUSTUS: Think, Faustus, upon God, that made the world.
MEPHOSTOPHILIS: Remember this—
FAUSTUS: Ay, go, accursèd spirit to ugly hell.
 'Tis thou hast damned distressèd Faustus' soul.
 Is't not too late?

(6.67–78)

It is definitely too late, and I wonder at the exegetes who debate the supposedly relevant theologies—Catholic, Calvinist, Lutheran—and their presumed effect upon whether Faustus either will not or cannot repent. Marlowe is no more interested in letting Faustus escape than in giving the wretched Edward II a good death. The play's glory is in the last speech of Faustus, an extraordinary rhapsody whose sixty lines form one of the great dramatic poems in the language. All of it is magnificent and subtle, but the final line almost transcends Faustus and his situation:

I'll burn my books!—Ah, Mephostophilis!

To burn his books of magic or Hermetic knowledge would be to burn himself, for he has become what he desired to become, his daemonic books. That "Ah, Mephostophilis!" spoken to the spirit who leads him off the stage is a sigh of surrender, a realization that, like Mephostophilis, he goes, after all, of his own accord and not just because he is summoned. We are not much moved by this damnation, any more than Marlowe could be much moved. Barabas has an extraordinary personality, and so in very different ways do Tamburlaine and Edward II. Doctor Faustus is scarcely a person and so hardly a personality at all. He is Marlowe's victim or scapegoat, sacrificed in Marlowe's own Black Mass, so as to utter a gorgeous, broken music in his demise. Simon Magus, the original Faustus, was a sublime charlatan; the nihilistic genius of Marlowe was content at the end with a merely eloquent charlatan.

Five-Act Structure in *Doctor Faustus*

G. K. Hunter

The original and substantive texts of Marlowe's *Doctor Faustus* (the Quartos of 1604 and 1616) present the play completely without the punctuation of act division or scene enumeration. This is common enough in the play-texts of the period. Indeed it is much the commonest form in plays written for the public theatres. Shakespeare's *Henry V* and *Pericles* are without divisions In their quarto texts, but we know that they were written with a five-act structure in mind—the choruses tell us that.

What is exceptional in the textual history of *Doctor Faustus* is not the lack of division in the original texts; it is rather the reluctance of modern editors to impose an act-structure on the modern texts. This is curious, but it seems possible to discern why the reluctance exists and a survey of the modern editions of *Faustus* throws some interesting light on critical attitudes to the subject matter of the play.

Marlowe (like other Elizabethan dramatists) was "rediscovered" by the educated English public in an atmosphere which played down his specifically dramatic and theatrical powers. Charles Lamb's *Specimens of the English dramatic poets who lived about the time of Shakespeare* (1808) established him primarily as a poet. This, as I say, did not distinguish him from other dramatists of the period. But the attitudes implied by Lamb's volume were more difficult to shake off in the case of *Doctor Faustus* than in other Elizabethan plays; for here they were reinforced, later in the century, by a second wave of anti-theatrical (or at least a-theatrical) influence. In 1887 the young Havelock Ellis (then a medical

From *Dramatic Identities and Cultural Tradition: Studies in Shakespeare and His Contemporaries*. © 1978 by G. K. Hunter. Barnes & Noble Books, 1978.

student) suggested to Henry Vizetelly, well known in "advanced" circles as a courageous though rather risqué publisher, that he should put out a series of unexpurgated (key word!) texts of the Elizabethan dramatists— the famous "Mermaid" series. The *Marlowe,* the first volume in the series, was edited by Ellis himself, and may be taken as a manifesto of the whole new movement. It bore proudly on the title-page the legend *Unexpurgated,* not simply because the usual casual indecencies of clown conversations were preserved, but rather because an appendix carried the full testimony of the informer Richard Baines "concernynge [Marlowe's] damnable opinions and judgment of Religion and scorne of Gods worde," to which Ellis added the even more offensive comment that such "damnable opinions . . . have, without exception, been substantially held, more or less widely, by students of science and the Bible in our own days." To say this of remarks like "Moses was but a juggler," "that Christ better deserved to die than Barabas," etc., was to push Marlowe into the front line of the late Victorian battle against bourgeois values. Marlowe appears as a social rebel and religious freethinker (like Ellis himself) and this comes to reinforce the earlier view that he was primarily a poet. The two attitudes join together, in fact, to suggest that he was a poet *because* he was a freethinker, rejecting social conventions in order to achieve his individual and personal vision. He becomes the morning-star of the 1890s, a harder and more gem-like Oscar Wilde.

In order to preserve the image of Marlowe as a cult-figure of this kind it is necessary to discount the theatrical, and so popular, provenance of his work. If he was the laureate of the atheistical imagination, he must have stood at a considerable distance from his rudely Christian audience; and this assumption presses especially heavily upon *Doctor Faustus,* whose hero is himself a freethinker and (by implication at least) a poet. It is not surprising therefore to find Ellis saying in his headnote to *Faustus:* "I have retained the excellent plan introduced by Professor Ward and adopted by Mr. Bullen, of dividing the play into scenes only; it is a dramatic poem rather than a regular drama." In the face of this critical assurance, and with the *Zeitgeist* exerting the kind of pressure that I have described, the earlier editorial practice of presenting the play in five acts, derived from the 1663 Quarto by Robinson (1826) and continued in Cunningham (1870), Wagner (1877), and Morley (1883), withered away. It was not until the bibliographical breakthrough of Boas, Kirschbaum, and Greg (1932, 1946, 1950) that the play reappeared in the five-act form. (I mean the perception that the 1616 text must be the basis of any modern recension. In this text the nature of the structure is much clearer; and it was, in fact, the reading of Greg's *editio minor* that first made clear to me the precision with which the play moved. Greg himself, however, hedges his bets. He finds the act division "convenient in discussing the construction of the play" and so presents it to the reader; but he confides to us in a footnote that "I see no reason to suppose that any act division was originally contemplated." His argument is that there is too great a disproportion between the numbers of lines to be found in the different acts for these to make just divisions. A rereading of *The Winter's Tale,* in which act 4 is two and a half times as long as act 3, ought to convince us of the peculiarity of this mode of assessment. It may be, of course, that Shakespeare also ought to be presented without act-division. But no editor has yet had the courage to present his text in this way.) Even after their labours the old attitudes persist. The edition by Kocher (1950) is divided into scenes only, and the recent replacement of Boas by the "Revels" edition of J. D. Jump (1962) avoids the act divisions: "Neither A1 [1604] nor B1 [1616] makes any attempt to divide the play into acts and scenes, so no such distribution is given prominence in the present edition." It may be sufficient reply to this to quote the recent comment of W. T. Jewkes, who has analysed the act structure of all the plays in the period:

> The plays of the "University wits," however, appear both undivided and divided. On a closer inspection it was evident that the clearly divided texts from this group were those which showed least sign of playhouse annotation, while those which retained fragmentary division, or none at all, showed signs of adaptation for performance. It is evident then that these dramatists divided their plays originally, but that adaptation for the stage resulted in either the total or partial loss of act headings.
>
> (*Act Division in Elizabethan and Jacobean Plays, 1583–1616*)

This argument might well be augmented, in the particular case of *Doctor Faustus,* by reference to the choruses which mark the beginnings of some of the acts, or by repeating Boas's observations about the material taken from the Faustbook. But it is not my purpose here to argue in detail the textual or theatrical probability that *Faustus* is in five-act form. I rather wish to look at the developing movement of the play to see if the act divisions accepted by Boas and others correspond to anything in the inner economy of the work, marking progressive stages in an organized advance through the material. Since Goethe remarked, "How greatly is it all planned" in 1829, many have been found to repeat his encomium, but few to justify it. I would suggest that the play *is* planned greatly, even precisely, in five clear stages (or acts), moving forward continuously in a single direction. I am assuming, when I say this, that the text as we have it in the 1616 Quarto is the product of a unified organizing intelligence. Marlowe *may* have had a collaborator, but I do not believe that we can detect his work—and a stroke of Occam's razor makes him disappear.

The first point I should like to make is that the action (I deal only with the main plot at the moment) moves through clearly separable stages. Act 1 is concerned (as is usual) with setting up the situation and introducing the principal characters. Here we learn the nature of Faustus's desires, set against the limiting factor of his nature; we meet Mephistophilis and the contrast between the two is made evident. Act 2 begins with a preliminary reminder (found before each act of the play) of the stage at which the action has arrived:

> Now Faustus must thou needs be damned,
> And canst thou not be saved.
> What boots it then to think on God or heaven?
> (2.1.1–3)

In act 1, the temptation to think of heaven is hardly present; but the subject here announced is the warp on which much of the main-plot action of act 2 is woven. The conflict is now entered upon in real earnest. The introductory note to act 3 is more obvious, being handled by the "Chorus." He tells us that "Learned Faustus," having searched into the secrets of Astronomy, now is gone to prove Cosmography. He is in fact completing his Grand Tour when we meet him, having taken in Paris, Mainz, Naples, Venice, and Padua, and is newly arrived in Rome, "Queen of the Earth" as Milton's Satan calls it, and the summation of worldly grandeur. Mephistophilis describes the sights, and then conducts his master into the highest social circles in the city, and so in the world.

Act 3 is spent in Rome; act 4 in the courts of Germany. The introductory Chorus makes clear the distinction between "the view / Of rarest things" which is the substance of act 3 and the "trial of his art" which is what we are to see in act 4. The introductory speech to act 5 is spoken by Wagner, Faustus's servant, who is confused in one text with the Chorus, and who is exercising here what is clearly a choric function. His first line marks the change of key: "I think my master means to die shortly." Act 5 is concerned with preparations and prevarications in the face of death.

It is obvious enough, I suggest, that each act handles a separate stage in Faustus's career. But it is not obvious from what I have said that the stages move forward in any single and significant line of development. To see that they do requires a fairly laborious retracing of the action, seen now in the light of what was more obvious to Marlowe and his audience than to us—the supposed hierarchy of studies.

The opening lines of the play show us Faustus trying to *settle his studies;* the opening speech, with this aim in mind, moves in an orthodox direction through the academic disciplines, beginning with logic, here representative of the whole undergraduate course of Liberal Arts, through the *Noble Sciences* of Medicine and Law and so to the *Queen of Sciences,* Divinity. So far, the movement has been, as I say, completely orthodox, and a frame of reference has been neatly established. But, having reached Divinity, Faustus still hopes to advance, and can only do so in reverse:

> Divinity, adieu!
> These metaphysics of magicians
> And negromantic books are heavenly.
> (1.1.49–51)

(I preserve the original form *negromantic,* though most modernizing editors change it to *necromantic.* This seems to me to be a greater change than is warranted by a licence to modernize. It is the "black art" in general that Faustus is welcoming, not the power to raise the dead.)

At this point he passes, as it were, through the looking glass; he goes on trying to evaluate experience, but his words of value (like "heavenly") now mean the opposite of what they should. The "profit and delight . . . power . . . honour . . . omnipotence" that he promises himself through the practice of magic are all devalued in advance. By embracing negromancy he ensures that worthwhile ends cannot be reached; and the rest of the play is a demonstration of this, moving as it does in a steadily downward direction.

The route taken by Faustus in his descent through human activities was, I think, intended to be easily understood by the original audience, and again I suggest that it is the structure of knowledge as at that time understood that provides the key. Divinity was, as I have noted, the "Queen of the Sciences." Not only so, but it was the discipline which gave meaning to all other knowledge and experience. Hugh of St Victor expresses the idea succinctly: "All the natural arts serve divine science, and the lower order leads to the higher." In Marlowe's own day the same point is made, more elaborately, in the popular *French Academy* of La Primaudaye:

> What would it availe or profit us to have and attaine unto the knowledge and understanding of all humane and morall Philosophy, Logicke, Phisicke, Metaphisicke, and Mathematick . . . not to bee ignorant of any thing, which the liberall arts and sciences teach us, therewith to content the curious minds of men and by that means to give them a tast, and to make them enjoy some kind of transitory good in this life: and in the meane time to be altogether and wholy ignorant, or badly instructed, in the true and onely science of divine Philosophy, whereat all the rest ought to aime.
>
> (Preface to book 4)

But if one rejects the final cause here supposed, what happens to the rest of knowledge? This is the question that the play asks and pursues. In what direction does the Icarus of learning fall when he abandons the orthodox methods of flight? The order of topics in the medieval encyclopaedias gives one some clue here. These regularly begin with God and divine matters. Vincent of Beauvais's *Speculum* starts from the Creator, then moves to "the empyrean heaven and the nature of angels," then to "the formless material and the making of the world; the nature and the properties of things created," then to the human state and its ramifications. The *De Rerum Natura* attributed to Bede and William of Conches's *Philosophia Mundi* have the same four-book order. Book 1 deals with God; book 2 with the heavens; book 3 with the lower atmosphere; book 4 with the earth, so down to man and his human activities. The *Proem* to book 4 (identical in both works) gives a fair indication of the nature of the movement assumed:

> The series of books which began with the First Cause has now descended to The Earth, not catering for itching ears nor loitering in the minds of fools, but dealing with what is useful to the reader. For now is that verse fulfilled: "For the time will come when they will not endure sound doctrine; but after their own lusts shall they heap to themselves teachers, having itching ears." (2 Timothy, iv, 3). But since the mind of the honest man does not turn after wickedness, but conforms itself to the better way, let us turn to the remaining subjects, in the

interest of a mind of this kind, estranged from wickedness and conformable to virtue.

In Marlowe's own day this order of topics appeared in works as popular as the Baldwin-Palfreyman *Treatise of Moral Philosophy* (innumerable editions from 1557 to 1640), in Palfreyman's companion *Treatise of Heavenly Philosophy*, and in William Vaughan's *The Golden Grove* (1600, 1608). *The French Academy,* which Marlowe has been supposed to have known, uses the same organization of topics but treats them in reverse order, upwards from (1) "the institution of manners and callings of all estates," through (2) "concerning the soule and body of man," and (3) "a notable description of the whole world . . . Angels . . . the foure elements . . . fowles, fishes, beasts . . ." etc. to (4) "Christian philosophy, instructing the true and onely meanes to eternall life." It seems reasonable to suppose that Marlowe knew this system of knowledge; and it is my assertion that he used it to plan the relationship of the parts of *Doctor Faustus.*

When Faustus has signed away his soul, the first fruits of his new "power . . . honour . . . omnipotence" appear in the knowledge of astronomy that he seeks. Astronomy is a heavenly art, no doubt—it appears early in the encyclopaedias—but it is one that is not obviously dependent on divinity. Yet here it leads by the natural process that the encyclopaedists describe to the question of first cause. If the heavens involve more than the tedium of mechanics ("these slender questions Wagner can decide") then astronomy leads straight back to the fundamental question: Who made the world? But, under the conditions of knowledge that Faustus has embraced, this basic question cannot be answered, for it is "against our kingdom." The trap closes on the pseudo-scholar and forces him backwards and downwards.

This is the movement—backwards into ever more superficial shallows of knowledge and experience—which continues inexorably throughout the whole play, as it must, given the initial choice. Baulked in act 2 from the full pursuit of astronomy, in act 3 Faustus turns to cosmography, from the heavens to the earth. But the charms of sightseeing pall, and a magical entrée even to the "best" society in the world involves only a tediously superficial contact. Marlowe's age had serious doubts about the importance of cosmography (or geography) as an object of human endeavour. *The French Academy* treats it under the heading of "curiosity and novelty," as a destructively unserious pursuit. The drop in the status of Faustus's activities is nicely caught by the change of tone between the Chorus at the beginning of act 3 and that introducing act 4. The first tells us that

> Learnèd Faustus
> To find the secrets of astronomy
> Graven in the book of Jove's high firmament
> Did mount him up to scale Olympus' top.
> (3.Prol.1–4)

We seem here still to be dealing with a genuine search for knowledge. But in the later chorus we hear only that

> When Faustus had *with pleasure* ta'en the view
> Of rarest things and royal courts of kings,
> He stay'd his course and so returnèd home.
> (4.Prol.1–3; my italics)

The emphasis is no longer on the search after knowledge, with discovery, presumably, as the aimed-for end, but with what is more appropriate to the diabolical premise ("that is not against our kingdom"), with pleasure taken and then given up, without reaching forward to the final causes. Faustus's merry japes among the cardinals are enjoyed by the protagonist, and are clearly meant to be enjoyed by the audience; but nothing more than pleasure is involved, and given the giant pretensions of the first act, the omission is bound to be a factor in our view of the Roman scenes.

Faustus not only views Rome. He also dabbles in statecraft, rescuing the Antipope Bruno and transporting him back to his supporters in Germany. The step from cosmography to statecraft is similar to that from astronomy to cosmography. In each case we have a reduction in the area covered, and an increasing remoteness from first causes. The panoply of state is not here (as it usually is in Shakespeare) an awesome and a righteous thing. It is not approached through the lives of those who must live and suffer inside the system, but via the structure of knowledge, so that it is the relationship to divinity rather than the power over individual lives that is the determining factor in our attitude. The ludicrous antics at the Papal court have usually been seen as a simple piece of Protestant propaganda, pleasing to the groundlings and inserted for no better reason. Yet one can see that this episode (placed where it is) has its own unique part to play in the total economy of the work. It is proper to start Faustus's descent through the world from the highest point, in Rome; it is equally proper to begin his social and political descent with the Vicar of Christ (and so down to Emperor, to Duke, and back to private life). By turning the conduct of the papal court into farce Marlowe devalues *all* sovereignty and political activity in advance. Bruno (and his tiara) are saved; but there is no suggestion that *he* has any more virtue to recommend him; he has no real function in the play except to reduce the title and state of the Pope to a mere name.

There is no suggestion in this act that Faustus himself is aware of the startling discrepancy between the actual happenings and the promises he made to himself (and to us) at the beginning of the play. The audience, however, can hardly forget so soon; and our memory is reinforced in the papal palace by the ritual threats of damnation uttered by the Pope and friars. It is no doubt comic that the Pope should be boxed on the ear and exclaim, "Damn'd be this soul for ever for this deed," but we should not fail to notice the sinister echo reverberating behind the horseplay; the curse is comic at this point, but sinister in the context of the whole action.

Act 4 carries the descent of Faustus one more clear step, by still further reducing the importance of the area in which he operates. I have mentioned the social descent to the secular courts of Emperor and Duke of Vanholt. At the same time there is a descent in terms of the kind of activity that the magic procures. Faustus's anti-Papal activities can be seen as political action of a kind, and this aspect would be more obvious to the Elizabethans than it is to us (involved, as they were, in the kind of struggle depicted). But in act 4 he is presented quite frankly as a court entertainer or hired conjurer. In the court of Charles V, of course, there is still some intellectual dignity in his activities. Charles's longing, to see "that famous conqueror, Great Alexander, and his paramour," is a kingly interest in a paragon of kingship. But when Faustus goes on to the court of the Duke of Vanholt he is reduced to satisfying nothing more dignified than the pregnant "longings" of the duchess for out-of-season grapes. At the same time his side activities are brought down by a parallel route. At the court of the Emperor he was matched against the disbelieving knights, Frederick, Benvolio, etc.; at Vanholt his opponents are clowns, the Horse-courser, the Hostess.

The last act of *Faustus* is often thought of as involving restoration of dignity and brilliance to the sadly tarnished magician. In terms of poetic power there is something to be said on this side; but the poetry that Faustus is given in this act serves to do more than simply glorify the speaker. The fiery brilliance of the Helen speech is lit by the Fire of Hell (as has been pointed out by Kirschbaum and others). The imminence of eternal damnation gives strength and urgency to the action, but the actions that Faustus himself can initiate are as trivial and as restricted as one would expect, given the moral development that I have described as operating throughout the rest of the play. There is no change of direction. In acts 3 and 4 we saw Faustus sink steadily from political intrigue at the Curia to fruit-fetching for a longing duchess. The last act shows a consistent extension of this movement. It picks up the role of Faustus as entertainer, but reduces the area of its exercise still further; it is now confined to the enjoyment of some "two or three" private friends, and as an epilogue to what Wagner characterizes by "banquet . . . carouse . . . swill . . . belly-cheer." Helen appears, in short, at the point where one might have expected dancing-girls.

The nature of the object conjured in act 5, no less than the occasion of the conjuring, shows the same logical development of the movement in the preceding acts. Charles V had longed to satisfy an intellectual interest; the Duchess of Vanholt longed for the satisfaction of a carnal but perfectly natural appetite; but the desire to view Helen of Troy is both carnal and (as the ironic word *blessed* should warn us) reprehensible, and leads logically to the further and final depravity of:

> One thing, good servant, let me crave of thee
> To glut the longing of my heart's desire—
> That I may have unto my paramour
> That heavenly Helen which I saw of late,
> Whose sweet embracings may extinguish clear
> Those thoughts that do dissuade me from my vow
> And keep mine oath I made to Lucifer.
>
> (5.1.90–96)

The circle in which Faustus conjures has now shrunk from the *urbs et orbis* of Rome to the smallest circle of all. When the dream of power was lost, the gift of entertainment remained; but even this has now faded. The conjuring here exists for an exclusively self-interested and clearly damnable purpose. The loneliness of the damned, summed up in Mephistophilis's cryptic *"Solamen miseris socios habuisse doloris"*—this now is clearly Faustus's lot. Left alone with himself and the mirror of his own damnation in Helen ("Her lips suck forth my soul: see where it flies!"), he is in a situation that cannot be reached by either the Old Man or the students. His descent has taken him below the reach of human aid; and there is a certain terrible splendour in this, as the poetry conveys, but the moral level of this splendour is never in doubt; it is something that the whole weight of the play's momentum presses on our attention, moving steadily as it does, through the clearly defined stages of its act-structure, away from the deluded dream of power and knowledge and downward, inevitably, coherently, and logically, into the sordid reality of damnation.

I have sought to show that the movement of the main plot of *Faustus* is controlled and splendidly meaningful. It moves in a single direction (downwards) through a series of definite stages which it would be wilfully obscurantist not to call acts. Indeed it conforms, by and large, to the strict form of five-act structure which was taught in Tudor grammar schools, out of the example of Terence. The structural paradigm was, of course, concerned with comedy, and especially the comedy of intrigue, and could not be applied very exactly to a moralistic tragedy like *Faustus*. But it is easy to see that act 1 of *Faustus* gives us the introductory materials, act 2 the first moves in the central conflict (Faustus versus the Devil), acts 3 and 4 the swaying back and forward of this conflict, and act 5 the catastrophe.

What is more, these stages of the main plot are reinforced or underlined by a parallel movement going on simultaneously in the subplot. The general relation between the two levels of the plot, the level of spiritual struggle and that of carnal opportunism, is one of parody—a mode of connection that was common in the period. And I should state that by "parody" I do not mean the feeble modern reduction of characteristics to caricature, but rather that multiple presentation of serious themes which relates them both to the man of affairs and to the light-minded clown.

It is not only in the detail of individual scenes that the subplot parodies the main plot: the whole movement of the subplot mirrors that social and intellectual descent that I have traced in the career of Faustus. The first subplot scene concerns Wagner, a man close to Faustus himself. The second comic scene involves Wagner and *his* servants, Robin and Dick. The third and subsequent scenes show Robin and Dick by themselves, Wagner having disappeared (he reappears—though not as part of the subplot—in 5.1). It has been argued [by F. S. Boas] that this very descent, and the disappearance of Wagner, "suggests a different hand" [*not Marlowe's*] for the Robin and Dick scenes. This provides an interesting parallel to the assumption that Marlowe cannot be responsible for the main-plot scenes in the middle of the play. At both levels the action descends to trivialities, and the critics close their eyes in dissent. But if the movement is deliberate at one level it seems likely that it is so at the other level also.

Even more impressive than this general movement in the subplot is the accumulation of details in which the action of the subplot scene mir-

Doctor Faustus's Sin

Wilbur Sanders

Just as, in the treatment of the supernatural order, Marlowe seems to
waver between a rather leaden-footed literalism and real imaginative insight, so in the characterisation of the sin for which Faustus is ultimately
damned, he seems uncertain of his ground. At times it is seen homilet-
ically as mere presumptuous pride, "a devilish exercise." At times (as it
acquires a real dramatic weight and body) it is seen, less simply, as a
legitimate aspiration somehow tainted at its source. And at times it is
simply endorsed with a kind of naïve enthusiasm which is very like the
wide-eyed wonderment of the *Faustbook*.

It is this uncertainty, I think, that has encouraged critics like Professor Ellis-Fermor to see Faustus's sin as a harmless variety of humanist
aspiration (for her, Marlowe the humanist is obliged to damn his hero
only because he has been guilty of intellectual apostasy in the face of a
menacing orthodoxy). This is to respond to something which is certainly
present in the play; but it is something of which the play is not, so to
speak, aware.

We have seen already [elsewhere] how Faustus's exploratory urges
could be taken to symbolise the intellectual expansionism of the Renaissance; and it is true that many even of his power fantasies are connected
with the widening geographical and mental horizons of that period: true
for instance that he proposes to "search all corners of the new-found
world." But for what? "For pleasant fruits and princely delicates" (1.83).
Helen may be the paradigm of classical beauty, the resuscitated body of

---

From *The Dramatist and the Received Idea: Studies in the Plays of Marlowe & Shakespeare*.
© 1968 by Cambridge University Press.

antique learning, but she is raised in order to become Faustus's paramour, and to "extinguish clear / Those thoughts that do dissuade me from my vow" (18.94). Indeed, most of Faustus's "humanist" impulses, closely scrutinised, resolve themselves into a familiar and explicit form of hedonism and epicurean self-indulgence. There is no doubt that Marlowe sets out to place very firmly the damnable nature of Faustus's ambition; and if we are to allow any force at all to Ellis-Fermor's mitigating contentions, we must do so by positing a Marlowe divided against himself, here as elsewhere. In fact, I believe, he was. But it is necessary, first of all, to see how hard he worked to show us the dangers of the Faustian path.

When one considers Faustus's motives for taking up the magical arts, it becomes clear that Marlowe wants us to detect a serious moral weakness at the root of the decision. There is, for instance, his contempt for the laborious particularity of the academic disciplines—"too servile and illiberal for *me*": the revealing stress on the personal pronoun ("Thou art too ugly to attend on *me*") is the dramatic embodiment of the psychological state which Marlowe sees to be attendant on such an intellectual attitude. Faustus prefers the grandiose cult of universals: he will "level at the end of every art." But there must be no hard work: the drudgery is to be deputed to his "servile spirits" (1.96). The irksome burden of unanswered questions can be shrugged off, for the spirits will "resolve me of all ambiguities" (1.79); and it's a desire for the fruits of knowledge without its pains which makes him long to "see hell and return again safe" (6.172). He shares that perennial human conviction that there's a short cut of knowledge, some formula that makes it unnecessary to go about and about the hill of truth—a conviction that is aptly symbolised in the delusions of magic. The art into which the two infamous magicians initiate him is one of those reassuring skills which demand exactly the knowledge one possesses—astrology, tongues, mineralogy (1.137)—yet promise immediate and infallible results. Cornelius and Valdes are the direct ancestors of our Pelmanists and Scientologists, and Faustus has plainly been reading their illustrated brochure when he remarks,

> Their conference will be a greater help to me
> Than all my labours, plod I ne'er so fast.
> (1.67)

It is plain, then, in the opening scenes, that Marlowe is giving us a portrait of an egocentric abuse of knowledge; Faustus belongs to that class of scholars who are, in Nashe's words, ambitious, haughty, and proud, nor do they loue vertue for it selfe any whit, but because they would ouerquell and outstrip others with the vaineglorious ostentation of it. A humour of monarchising and nothing els it is, which makes them affect rare quallified studies.

It is certainly a desire for "vaineglorious ostentation" which makes Faustus aspire to the status of an Agrippa, "whose shadows made all Europe honour him" (1.116). "Be a physician Faustus," he advises himself, "and be eterniz'd for some wondrous cure" (1.14—the vaguely indefinite "some" is an index of the extent to which aspiration is divorced from reality, while "eterniz'd" reminds us how constantly Faustus makes his felicity reside in the mouths of men). For such an academic megalomaniac, the triumphant university disputation is the most delectable of memories:

> I . . . have with concise syllogisms
> Gravell'd the pastors of the German church,
> And made the flowering pride of Wittenberg
> Swarm to my problems as the infernal spirits
> On sweet Musaeus when he came to hell.
>
> (1.111)

It is with such relish that he finds himself able to equate Wittenberg's "flowering pride" with a swarm of infernal bees! And the relish is there because he has set all his pleasure upon the subjugation of other beings to his personal gratification. But this is an appetite which reasserts itself at the very moment of its satisfaction; for, once subjugated, the divines of Wittenberg can no longer minister to his sense of power, and he must go in search of increasingly larger spheres in which to exercise his passion for domination. Which is the plot of the play.

If there is one key motif in the scenes leading up to the signing of the pact, it is this "humour of monarchising," an obsessive preoccupation with power: power over the grand forces of nature—winds, storms (1.57), the Rhine (1.88), the ocean (3.41), the air (3.107); power over national and international destinies ("The Emperor shall not live but by my leave, / Nor any potentate of Germany"—3.112 and cf. 1.86, 91–95); power over the storehouses of nature ("I'll have them fly to India for gold, / Ransack the ocean for orient pearl"—1.81 and cf. 1.74, 143–46), over the plate-fleets of Spain (1.130); even the disposition of the continental land-masses (3.109–10) and the movements of the celestial bodies (3.40) are to be at his command. Those of his dreams which are not merely anarchistic nihilism—as the ocean overwhelming the world, the moon dropping from her sphere (3.40–41) or the petty prosecution of private revenge (3.98)—are simply variations on a single theme: "I'll be great emperor of the world" (3.106). His mind, like Epicure Mammon's, thrown into near delirium at the prospect, casts up this strange farrago of preposterous fantasies in the future tense ("I'll . . . I'll . . . I'll . . ."). Like Mammon, too, Faustus earns our contempt by assuming that the beings of superior power with whom he traffics exist merely to gratify his whims.

Such ambitions are not only damnable, they are laughable, and in terms of the chosen peripateia they are clearly to be regarded as arrant folly and presumption. But Marlowe, we recall, is the author of *Tamburlaine* (*Tamburlaine* the indulgence *ad absurdum* of the "humour of monarchising," not the moral fable critics have made out of it). And the more I look at the verse in which Faustus's grandiose visions are expounded the less certain I am that Marlowe has wholly dissociated himself from his hero—any more than the anonymous author of the *Faustbook* had done. In both the play and its source book, there are long stretches where a naïve wonder at the subtleties of the witch completely submerges the moral condemnation of witchcraft—an ambiguity which results from the shallowness of the initial condemnation. At such points in the play (and I would include nearly all the central section, scenes 8–17, under this heading) the verse is strangely neutral morally—Mammon's foamings at the mouth provide an instructive contrast—has no clearly placed tone, only a shallow fluency and prolixity that suggest it came a trifle too easily to its author. It is neither the clear moral evaluation of a diseased mind, nor the enactment of a kindling imagination, but the indulgence of an abiding mood or mode in Marlowe's rhetorical poetic.

This becomes clear if we consider one passage where we do get a genuine presentation of the quickened pulse and soaring imagination of a man awestruck before a new universe of meaning and potentiality:

> O, what a world of profit and delight
> Of power, of honour, of omnipotence,
> Is promis'd to the studious artisan!
> All things that move between the quiet poles
> Shall be at my command: emperors and kings
> Are but obey'd in their several provinces,
> Nor can they raise the wind or rend the clouds;

> But his dominion that exceeds in this
> Stretcheth as far as doth the mind of man.
>
> (1.52)

By charting so subtly the accumulating emotion behind the words, this masterfully articulated crescendo gives to the word "dominion" a richer and more human meaning than it has elsewhere. "Power" in these terms is not merely a presumptuous aspiration beyond the human condition, but a very nearly legitimate ambition closely, though ambiguously, related to the passion for mastery that leads to knowledge and "truth." If this vein had been more diligently uncovered in the rest of the play, we might have had a tragedy. But even this fine passage is immediately followed by a piece of rant in the Tamburlaine vein, which tips the delicate balance between an imaginative sympathy which is itself a judgment, and a top-heavy moral censure:

> A sound magician is a demi-god;
> Here tire, my brains, to get a deity!

The overstrain in the verse—expressing itself here in a syntactical incoherence—is not, I suggest, a dramatisation of Faustus's mental state. It is too imprecise and too hectic to be that. Rather it is Marlowe forcing an insurrectionary line of thought to discredit itself by overprotestation. Again, awareness of a tormenting ambivalence at the heart of all speculation, unsatiable or otherwise, has given way to flat homiletic demonstration.

The element of demonstration is strong in *Faustus*—most notably in the rejection of learning which opens the action. Faustus here indulges in a conventional, if not an academic, exercise: the "Dispraise of Learning." But both his methods and his conclusions are strikingly different from the Christianised pyrrhonism of his models. Faustus does not, in the traditional manner, indicate the shortcomings of human wit by showing how far each science falls short of its own avowed aims, and how far of divine omniscience; nor does he conclude with an exhortation to study only to know oneself and God. Instead he refers all learning to his private satisfaction, and finishes by rejecting "divinity" along with the rest.

The startlingly egocentric nature of his rejection can be estimated by comparing a contemporary survey of the same area—Cornelius Agrippa's *De Incertitudine et Vanitate Scientarum.* Agrippa, like Faustus, has bidden *on kai me on* farewell; but for what reasons? Because the philosophers "striue and disagree among themselues in all things," one sect subverting another; because their reason "cannot perswade no constant or certaine thinge, but doth alwayes wauer in mutable opinions"; because Logic, the philosopher's tool, is "nothinge els, but a skilfulnes of contention and darknesse, by the whiche al other sciences are made more obscure, and harder to learne"; because their conclusions ground themselves upon authority where they should build upon experience. Here is Faustus surveying the same territory:

> Is to dispute well logic's chiefest end?
> Affords this art no greater miracle?
> Then read no more, *thou hast attain'd that end;*
> A greater subject fitteth Faustus' wit.
> Bid *on kai me on* farewell.
>
> (1.8)

The shifty way in which one section of philosophy (Logic) is equated with all of Aristotle, and then used to discredit philosophy itself, makes one doubt that there was ever a serious intellectual objection here at all.

Again, Agrippa has no time for Physic, which he finds to be "a certaine Arte of manslaughter . . . aboue the knowledge of the lawe," because it cannot predict what it claims to control, yet, unperturbed by this technological breakdown, makes increasingly extravagant claims for its efficacy. Faustus:

> The end of physic is our body's health.
> Why, Faustus, *hast thou not attain'd that end?*
> Is not thy common talk sound aphorisms?
> Are not thy bills hung up as monuments,
> Whereby whole cities have escap'd the plague
> And thousand desperate maladies been cured?
> Yet art thou still but Faustus, and a man.
>
> (1.17)

Of "the Lawe and Statutes" Agrippa complains that they are merely a compound of men's uncertain opinions, "altered at euerye chaunge of time, of the State, of the Prince," and cannot, consequently, represent any real principle of justice. For Faustus the disillusionment expounds itself in words like "petty" and "paltry." The failure of Law to realise in the temporal sphere the justice that humanity demands of the divine order is far from his mind:

> This study fits a mercenary drudge
> Who aims at nothing but external trash,
> Too servile and illiberal for me.
>
> (1.34)

In each of these cases, the rewards of learning are conceived entirely in terms of the recognition and acclaim which are accorded to the practitioner. Where Agrippa refers a science to the principles which it is supposed to embody, and finds it wanting, Faustus refers the whole body of human learning to his private satisfaction—"The god thou serv'st is thine own appetite"—and when he discovers, either that the offered satisfaction is already available to him, or that it is one he does not covet, he passes on. Agrippa is by no means a profound thinker: but beside Faustus's glib superficiality, Agrippa's carefree *a priori* pyrrhonism seems eminently sane.

Now it may be that we have here Faustus's mental history in a conventionalised form; but if so, it is the mental history of a shallow mind— a sophist's mind: and the telescoping of time (if that is what it is) has the dramatic effect of heightening the sense of shallowness. It is important to realise that the investigation is no more than a facade (note the tone of pert self-congratulation and the glib transitions—as if the books were all ready with the markers at the relevant pages), and that the real decision has been taken in the first four lines, where Faustus exhorts himself to "be a divine in show / Yet level at the end of every art." Divinity, of course, was the science which claimed to do just this, and Faustus has already made the "end of every art" antithetical to the study of God.

There is a peremptory haste about the whole sequence, punctuated as it is by the clap of shut books and the breathless snatching of the next ("Galen come . . . Where is Justinian? . . ."), and as a result, when the abrupt slackening of pace does come, it is doubly arresting:

> These metaphysics of magicians
> And necromantic books are heavenly;
> Lines, circles, letters, characters:
> Ay, these are those that Faustus most desires.
>
> (1.48—B text)

At once the factitious clouds of sophistry disperse, and, gloating over his symbolic hieroglyphs in irrational fascination, Faustus finds his true tone. The seriousness of his commitment to a thorough-going rationalism is indicated here by the interesting, though not surprising, fact that he does not apply the same rational canons to the "arte magick": it is enough that "these are those that Faustus most desires."

Faustus's condemnation is thus writ large (too large, as I see it) in the opening scene. In order to regard him as a premature Promethean hero of the Enlightenment, one must either regard all enlightened Prometheans as damnable (this is roughly Miss Mahood's position), or admit that, judged by enlightened criteria, he is a decidedly damp squib. In anybody's book the attitudes he adopts are unworthy.

And yet there is here that same absence of moral orientation of the *energies* of the verse, however loudly the attitudes expressed may call out for censure. As with the presentation of Faustus's power fantasies, there is an emotional indirection making it almost impossible to be sure that Marlowe has not gone a-whoring after the strange gods he appears to abominate. To a dangerous degree Faustus *is* Marlowe, and the play is a vehement attempt to impose order on a realm of consciousness which is still in insurrection.

Perhaps this is why Marlowe overdoes the condemnation. This frivolous academic opportunist, who has clearly learned very little from his encyclopedic education, cannot engage our sympathies very deeply. The narrow moral categories of the Prologue seem entirely adequate to encompass the significance of such a presumptuous fool:

> swollen with cunning of a self-conceit,
> His waxen wings did mount above his reach,
> And, melting, heavens conspir'd his overthrow.
> (Prologue, 20)

This is the tone and manner of homiletic demonstration, not of tragic paradox, and it is in harmony with the Faustus of the early scenes.

On the one hand, then, we have a conscious and studied rejection of Faustus's position, which phrases itself in explicit moral comment and in an only slightly less explicit ironic exposure of his dubious motivation. On the other hand, there is an unrecognised hankering after the pleasures of magic, which turn, as the play progresses, into something very like the pleasures of the senses—"all voluptuousness." This split in sensibility, between the conscious design and the subconscious desire, is a familiar strait of the Puritan imagination—which finds its illicit Comuses and Bowers of Bliss too powerfully attractive to be dealt with on any but a moralistic level. Yet the moralisation which promises to free the mind from the tyranny of the sensory, this theoretical world-negation, simply hides the secret appetites from sight, and sharpens them as it prohibits their gratification. Thus it gives rise simultaneously to moralistic excess, and to a hectic and unwholesome obsession with the lost joys of mere sensuality. As we shall see, it is a peculiarly protestant dilemma in more ways than one.

If there were no more than this in *Doctor Faustus,* it would not exercise the kind of fascination it does. But there is also a desperate fatalism about Marlowe's vision, a sense that all the most desirable and ravishing things, man's fulfilment itself, are subject to a cosmic veto. A tragic rift yawns between the things man desires as man, and the things he must be content with, as sinner. And it is partly against this dark fatality that Faustus mobilises his doomed revolt.

I have described the rejection of learning as peremptory and wilful. But there is one significant moment where Faustus is brought up short for a moment, darkly brooding over one of his texts; and because the subject of his contemplation introduces one of the most impressive movements in the play, it is worth examining the passage carefully.

> *Stipendium peccati, mors est:* ha, *stipendium,* etc.
> The reward of sin is death? that's hard:
> *Si pecasse negamus, fallimur, & nulla est in nobis veritas:*
> If we say that we have no sin
> We deceive ourselves, and there is no truth in us.
> Why then belike we must sin,
> And so consequently die,
> Ay, we must die, an everlasting death.
> What doctrine call you this? *Che sarà, sarà:*
> What will be, shall be; Divinity adieu.
> (1.39—B text punctuation and lineation)

Scholars have provided the biblically unlearned with the second halves of Faustus's texts—"but the gift of God is eternal life," and "if we confess our sins, he is faithful and just to forgive us our sins"—and we have been made aware that Faustus's argument only holds good in the absence of Grace. Paul Kocher has even unearthed an example of this precise syllogism, duly refuted by a theologian. Any member of Marlowe's audience, we gather, could have given this crude sophistry its logical quietus. And so he might; but whether he would thereby have been rid of the problem is another question.

For as the sixteenth century became the seventeenth, and as a distorted Calvinist theology grew increasingly vocal in English pulpits, the possibility of reprobation without appeal became one of the most earnestly discussed topics of English theology. In the year Marlowe took his B.A., the debate flared up as a Cambridge graduate and future archbishop, Samuel Harsnett, denounced the preachers of a reprobation which had, he claimed, "grown high and monstrous, and like a Goliath, and men do shake and tremble at it." Series of manuals offering to satisfy the reader about his election or otherwise were printed and reprinted. Cases of conscience like the famous one of Francis Spira, which may have influenced *Faustus,* encouraged unholy and obsessive speculation about one's eternal destiny. There was a distinct feeling in the air that, though damnation was a certainty unless steps were taken to avert it, salvation was a problematical and tricky business. And there is plenty of evidence to suggest that Marlowe at Cambridge was thoroughly exposed to this opinion and the debates it provoked.

It doesn't require much imagination to see how this kind of thinking, robed with all the grandeur of theological authority, might prey upon a mind already open to suggestions of guilt and worthlessness. Those who thought it necessary to preach against the doctrine were certainly aware of the savage self-contempt which it reinforced in unstable personalities.

But Faustus's syllogism is not simply a theological curiosity, nor is it a position to be rebutted and then forgotten. It has an alarming kind of internal and experiential logic which survives refutation. The predestinarian crux is the basilisk eye of Christianity. It proposes the desperate and totally destructive possibility, to which, in his blacker moments, man is prone to yield. Faustus is a little chirpy about it at first—"Why then belike we must sin, and so consequently die"—but he immediately feels the dark compulsion of the idea: "Ay, we must die, an everlasting death." It is the siren song of annihilation, inviting the guilt which is an inescapable component of personality to rise and engulf the whole being. Faustus reacts vigorously and, as I have said, peremptorily: "What doctrine call you this? . . . Divinity adieu." But in that brief brooding pause we have seen his rebellion from an angle which reveals it as, in some sense, a revolt *for life,* not against life. Magic is at least one way of escaping the gloomy pessimism of this doomed view of human existence. The essential pessimism of *Marlowe's* vision lies in the fact that magic is also, for the play, delusion.

It is, I suppose, fairly obvious that the deity of *Doctor Faustus* is not the God of Love, the Good Shepherd, but either the avenging Jehovah of the Old Testament, or his Christian offshoot, the Calvinist tyrant of mass reprobation. This God, in less troubled days, had been Tamburlaine's patron and protector:

> There is a God, full of revenging wrath,
> From whom the thunder and the lightning breaks,
> Whose scourge I am, and him will I obey.
> (2 *Tam*. 5.1.182)

In *Tamburlaine* this deity was transparently a theological "front" for a bloody-minded aggressiveness in the Scythian general, if not in Marlowe himself. But in the period between *Tamburlaine* and *Faustus,* complacent identification with this appalling God has given way to torment and horror before it. In a very real sense, *Faustus* is an unsuccessful attempt to evade the fatal embrace of this murderous and irresistible deity—Marlowe's attempt as well as Faustus's.

The escape route is remarkably congruent with what we know of Marlowe's own revolt, for Faustus's rebellion takes the shape of a flirtation with a kind of free-thought that was fairly widely disseminated in Renaissance Europe. He quesions the immortality of the soul (3.64); he asks, and apparently wants to be informed, about the origins of the world (though the form of this question labels him an incurable theist—6.69); he wonders whether hell exists, or if it does whether it has anything like the horrors depicted by the theologians (3.61–63; 5.116–40), and his scepticism has the characteristic Epicurean tinge that tended, in the sixteenth century, to go with the release of the "advanced thinker" from the oppression of threatened punishment—he wants to spend his "four-and-twenty years of liberty" "in all voluptuousness" (3.94 and 8.61).

But like that of most of the "atheist" rebels of this period, Faustus's free-thought is far from being untroubled. It is deeply involved with personal pressures, and still joined, by the umbilical cord of a terror-which-is-still-faith, to the theism it purports to reject.

Faustus's learned discussions with Mephostophilis, for instance, have a persistent and revealing tendency to finger the wound in his own consciousness—and this despite the fact that he is, ostensibly, searching for the new and startling truths which his liberation from old dogma should have freed him to contemplate:

> Are all celestial bodies but one globe
> As is the substance of this centric earth?
> (6.36)

When Mephostophilis proves to be stonily orthodox, he is not content, and raises the problem of the eccentric motion of the planets:

> But have they all
> One motion, both *situ et tempore*?

But again he is disappointed, for Mephostophilis merely falls back upon the hypothesis of the poles of the zodiac. His impatience is clear: "These slender questions Wagner can decide: / Hath Mephostophilis no greater skill? . . . These are freshman's suppositions." And again he circles nearer his objective:

> But, tell me, hath every sphere a dominion or *intelligentia*?

asking in effect, How true is the spiritual order allegedly governing the material universe? Here Mephostophilis is again reactionary, for the intelligences had already been expounded as metaphors for behaviour according to rational laws, yet he asserts their objective existence. (It is one of the play's most telling ironies that the new diabolic knowledge, for which Faustus sells his soul, should prove to be nothing more than the old scholastic cosmos which he has contemptuously rejected in its favour.)

There is a little more elementary astronomical catechising, which Mephostophilis answers conservatively, whereat Faustus concedes, "Well, I am answered," in a voice that implies he is not; then, precipitately, he rushes on to his true question:

> Now tell me who made the world.

This is his real point of attack; for it is the divinely created, providentially ordered universe that he is so reluctant to accept. The answer he receives is presented with tremendous dramatic force as an upheaval in hell. Mephostophilis refuses to answer, and his sullen recalcitrance grows into a menacing anger, so menacing that Faustus sees, for the first time since his original encounter with the demonic world, the repellent face of evil:

> Ay, go, accursed spirit, to ugly hell!

The fiend's abrupt departure and his subsequent return with Lucifer and Beelzebub at precisely the moment when Faustus calls upon Christ is, as James Smith points out, an apt representation of the emotional upheaval which the very asking of the question provokes in Faustus's consciousness. For his particular form of scepticism is accompanied by, perhaps derived from, a profound emotional involvement with the ideas he rejects; and if his atheism is superficial, it is superficial because his theism is ineradicable.

The same tension between attraction and repulsion is discernible in the exaggerated gestures with which he dismisses the "vain trifles of men's souls" (3.64), and the "old wives' tales" of an after-life (5.136), but especially in the ambiguous attitudes that he adopts towards hell itself. It is interesting to note that on this issue (the existence of hell) he also employs the same wary catechising technique, pouncing on discrepancies, and driving home with the question which he hopes will extort the desired information. When Mephostophilis declares himself to be "for ever damn'd with Lucifer," Faustus is immediately on the alert:

> Where are you damn'd?
> MEPHOSTOPHILIS: In hell.
> FAUSTUS: How comes it then that thou art out of hell?
> (3.76)

The fiend's answer has gone down in the annals of theatrical history, but its revelation of a hell that is co-extensive with the existence of mind is precisely the reverse of what Faustus was seeking: it was not hell, but the power of the sound magician, that was to stretch "as far as doth the mind of man." Yet Faustus is not answered: his view of hell continues to fluctuate wildly throughout the play.

That hell is "a fable" (5.128) is only one of the positions he adopts: if it is "sleeping, eating, walking and disputing," as Mephostophilis suggests, then he'll "willingly be damn'd" (5.139–40). On the one hand, he "confounds hell in Elysium"—meaning, I take it, that the two are a single state, the classical Hades where his ghost will be "with the old philosophers" (3.62–63); on the other hand, Mephostophilis is exhorted to "scorn those *joys* thou never shalt possess" (3.88) and Faustus acknowledges that he has "incurr'd *eternal death*" (3.90). It is only after he has asked for and received a description of hell from a being to whom he is talking only because he believes him to have come from hell, that Faustus declares hell to be a fable. Yet, a few scenes later, Lucifer's genial assurance that "in hell is all manner of delight" (6.171) sends him grovelling for a sight of the fabulous place.

But there's a deep consistency here. Hell is a fable only as long as it's a place "where we are tortur'd and remain forever." If it affords "all manner of delight," he believes in it. He'll scorn the joys he'll never possess only because he does not believe them to be joys. He'll willingly be damned provided he can have damnation on his own terms—"sleeping, eating, walking and disputing." The consistency resides in his determination to submit all moral categories to his personal convenience; and the ultimate failure of such an enterprise is figured in the continual presence of the melancholy fiend who knows better than to attempt it. On Mephostophilis's terms—being in hell and knowing it—one can be damned and preserve one's dignity; on Faustus's—being in hell and pretending it's heaven—one can only prevaricate and rationalise, writhing on the pin which holds one fast to an inexorably moral universe.

Moral systems can only be overthrown on moral grounds. What revolutions in morality humanity has seen, have all been conducted in the interests of some higher principle which has hitherto been overlooked. Faustus's reorganisation of morality can make no such claim; it aims merely at making the universe more convenient to live in—"if I may haue my desire while I liue, I am satisfied, let me shift after death as I may," as Robert Greene put it. It lacks even the Utilitarian grace of considering the convenience of mankind as a whole. It is Faustus's private revolution, the objectives of which would be utterly subverted if all men were to participate in its benefits. Marlowe draws with perception and firmness the disastrous blindness implicit in this epicurean individualism. One sees, in the scenes depicting Faustus's accommodation to damnation and the creed of hell, the kind of meaning that could be given to his rejection of the traditional wisdom: it is a rejection of the "communal" element in human endeavour; and one immediate result is a dangerous isolation which Marlowe dramatises in the long midnight colloquies with the non-human Mephostophilis.

Very often of course it is necessary to cut oneself off from the assumptions that come most easily; but equally often, the severing of bonds is succeeded by a servile commitment to the party that promises emancipation. In Faustus's case the commitment is to the nonhuman and for the greater part of the play he is shown trying to be "a spirit in form and substance," to the consequent atrophy of his specifically human potentialities. "He is not well with being over-solitary."

This is why his eleventh-hour return to the domestic limitations of the scholar's life, and his poignant reaching out for human contact, are so extraordinarily moving—at last his estranged and suppressed humanity has risen to demand its due. When the First Scholar regrets that Faustus has given his friends no opportunity to pray for him (19.69–70), he is speaking not only of the loss of divine grace, but also of the communal human support which men can give each other, from which Faustus, by his "singularity," has cut himself off.

It is when this doomed attempt at autarchy and self-signification collides with the demands of a nature still fundamentally religious, that the play again moves into a region of tragic potential:

> GOOD ANGEL: Faustus, repent; yet God will pity thee.
> BAD ANGEL: Thou art a spirit; God cannot pity thee.
> FAUSTUS: Who buzzeth in mine ears I am a spirit?
>   Be I a devil, yet God may pity me;
>   Yea, God will pity me if I repent.
> BAD ANGEL: Ay, but Faustus never shall repent.
>
> (6.12)

The Angels withdraw, leaving Faustus to the bottomless solitude of moral responsibility:

> My heart is harden'd, I cannot repent.
> Scare can I name salvation, faith, or heaven,
> But fearful echoes thunders in mine ears,
> 'Faustus, thou art damn'd!' Then guns and knives,
> Swords, poison, halters, and envenom'd steel
> Are laid before me to dispatch myself;
> And long ere this I should have done the deed
> Had not sweet pleasure conquer'd deep despair.
>
> (6.18)

Beneath the rhetorical symmetries of the Angels' speech lies the tragic paradox of a consciousness ruinously divided against itself—a consciousness powerfully drawn by "salvation, faith and heaven," yet deafened by the "fearful echoes" that thunder in his ears when he names them, by those magnified reverberations of his own despairing self-accusation. The sense of imprisonment within the self is so overwhelming that he can only frame it in terms of external coercion—"My heart is harden'd." To ask whether he is in fact coerced, or whether he only imagines he is, is meaningless. Unless we blind ourselves with a drastically over-simplified view of volition, we must recognise in Faustus's predicament a perennial human impasse.

The situation is given added depth as he goes on to specify the "sweet pleasure" in a way that transcends mere "voluptuousness" and becomes a passionate love of beauty:

> Have not I made blind Homer sing to me
> Of Alexander's love and Oenon's death?
> And hath not he, that built the walls of Thebes

> With ravishing sound of his melodious harp,
> Made music with my Mephostophilis?
> Why should I die, then, or basely despair?

Why indeed? The music is so entirely present in the lyric cadence of these lines that it becomes more than an infernal palliative. And the mention of Mephostophilis does not so much ironically discredit the vision, as transform the fiend into a sweet musician in consort with all the singers of antiquity. Faustus's religious consciousness, his desperate self-rejection, and his love of beautiful things, are here locked in internecine conflict, none prevailing yet none yielding. It is one of the finest moments in the play.

If one had to select a single scene as the imaginative heart of the action, I think it would be this one (scene 6), with its appalling and giddy oscillation between the profundities of despair and the escapist frivolities of the Pageant of the Sins; with its superb dramatisation of Faustus's love-hate relation with God, when he calls on Christ and is confronted by Lucifer. If he is torn more violently than this by his divided nature, he cannot survive.

But increasingly, from this point onwards, the hardness of heart, and the corresponding stiffness of mind, provide him with an assured resting place—"Now Faustus must / Thou needs be damn'd . . . Despair in God, and trust in Beelzebub" (5.1–5). He resolves the agonies of choice by falling back on an assumed external fate; and though he wavers and has to exhort himself to "be resolute," his resolution never takes cognizance of the contrary impulse towards repentance. The two are absolutely dissevered. He seems to prefer damnation; for, as a reprobate, he is in a position to exercise that limited variety of "manly fortitude" which consists in scorning the joys he never shall possess. His is the kind of mind which prefers consistency to integrity. He is stiff to maintain any purpose. And in that stiffness he goes to hell.

I have called this movement in the play (the movement concerned with Faustus's desperate attempt to defy a reality of his own nature) tragic, because it leads us beyond the homiletic framework of the opening scenes, and asks us to conceive of a conflict between immovable conviction and irresistible doubt on the battleground of the individual consciousness. At such moments, the evaluation of Faustus's moral condition is no longer possible in terms like the Chorus's "swollen with cunning of a self-conceit." Marlowe's attempt to impose order on his rebellion moves out of the sphere of moralistic abstraction into a world where the felt reality of the heavenly values constitutes their sole claim to serious attention.

And it is a basic element in Faustus's damnation that salvation and the means to it should never seem more than "illusions, fruits of lunacy." Although that salvation is a continual theoretical possibility, there is a blockage in Faustus's consciousness which makes "contrition, prayer, repentance" appear always to be unreal alternatives. And the blockage is Marlowe's too. Why else can it be that the heavenly can only be represented in the faint efflorescence of the Good Angel's utterances, or in the Old Man's appeal to a "faith" which claims will triumph over "vile hell" (18.124), but which is imprisoned within its own theological concepts? There is a crippling generality about the salvation the Old Man offers:

> I see an angel hovers o'er thy head
> And with a vial full of precious *grace*
> Offers to pour the same into the soul:
> Then call for *mercy,* and avoid *despair.*
> (18.61)

As spiritual counsel this is hopelessly inadequate, and the reply Marlowe gives Faustus—"I feel / Thy words to comfort my distressed soul"— seems forced and unconvincing.

The final declaration of Marlowe's failure to give body to the heavenly order is the creaking machinery of the descending "throne" in scene 19. The only face of God that we see—and see with frightening immediacy— is one from which Faustus recoils in horror:

> See where God
> Stretcheth out his arms and bends his ireful brows.
> Mountains and hills, come, come, and fall on me,
> And hide me from the heavy wrath of God!
> No, no.
> (19.150)

The conception of divine justice which prevails is Lucifer's—"Christ cannot save thy soul, for he is just" (6.87). Justice expresses itself in the total rejection and annihilation of "distressed Faustus."

Under the species of the nature of God, a man figures to himself the friendliness or hostility of the universe, and the possibilities of his existence within it. Marlowe's view of the matter appears to be black in the extreme. The play is permeated with a strong sense of man's alienation from the order of things, a deeply felt "sense of sin," which seems to dominate its vision. As J. B. Steane points out, the "lurking sense of damnation *precedes* the invocation" of hell.

It is in the sense that the world of the play is hostile to the only values that can redeem it that Faustus's damnation may be said to be imposed from above. Yet there is an urgency and a personal heat behind this terrible paradox which, though it defeats the synthesising activity of Marlowe's art, commands attention and, indeed, a regretful respect. Though the play's grasp of reality is sporadic, its reach is tremendous. We are watching a man, I suggest, locked in a death embrace with the agonising God he can neither reject nor love. It is the final consummation of the Puritan imagination.

Yet, though this may be the tragedy of Christopher Marlowe, it is not *The Tragicall History of Doctor Faustus*. The tragic dilemma we sense behind the play is *behind* it. It is not officially recognised as a powerful and autonomous insight of revolutionary import. Instead Marlowe tries to accommodate it, by means of the *psychomachia* form, to the old frontiers and boundaries of moralised experience. And it refuses to submit.

The apotheosis of Helen, for instance, which is supposed to be firmly placed as a narcotic which "may extinguish clear / Those thoughts that do dissuade" Faustus from his vow, nevertheless overflows the moral banks Marlowe is constructing.

> O, thou art fairer than the evening's air
> Clad in the beauty of a thousand stars,
> Brighter art thou than flaming Jupiter
> When he appear'd to hapless Semele,
> More lovely than the monarch of the sky
> In wanton Arethusa's azur'd arms,
> And none but thou shalt be my paramour.
> (18.112)

Up to this point, the image's sensual potency has been qualified by the destruction with which it is associated—"burnt," "sack'd," "combat," "wound"; but here the flame of passion flares up so fiercely that is transfigures even so moral an epithet as "wanton." The conflict is sharp in this scene, for these lines are immediately succeeded by the Old Man's

> Accursed Faustus, miserable man,
> That from thy soul exclud'st the grace of heaven
> And fliest the throne of his tribunal seat!
> (18.119)

It is clear that this comment cannot contain the Helen vision; but equally clear that Marlowe expects it to. The "humanist" and the moralist in him are again at war.

Thus Marlowe comes within hailing distance of that internalisation of moral sanctions by which drama can *lead* into wisdom instead of *pointing* at it, only to abandon it for easier simplifications:

> Faustus is gone: regard his hellish fall,
> Whose fiendful fortune may exhort the wise.

This, cheek by jowl with Faustus's last moments, is the critical paradox of the play at its most acute. I suppose it might be argued that the Epilogue merely condenses, into conventional and manageable form, a dramatic experience too vast and chaotic to be left unformulated; but I am inclined to think that the effect is simply bathetic.

Marlowe's *Doctor Faustus* and the Ends of Desire

Edward A. Snow

Perhaps the most difficult thing about writing on Marlowe is finding some way of formulating and discussing his themes that will not betray the radically questioning nature of his work. For instance, if we were forced to venture a statement about the central topic of *Doctor Faustus,* it would probably not be untrue to suggest that the play, like all of Marlowe's work, is about the fulfillment of will. Yet this would scarcely suggest the extent to which the play puzzles about what the will is, and what fulfillment consists of, and how words like "will," "want," and "have" can victimize the speaker who tries to make them serve his purposes. Every time the drama raises the issue of what Faustus wants, it does so in a way that subtly deflects attention away from the ostensible objects of his desire toward the ontological ambiguities at its origin. All of his specific desires, the more randomly and recklessly they accumulate, and the more compulsively he *speaks* of them, begin to seem mere epiphenomena, attempts to rationalize an alien, anxiously prior inward restlessness by creating around it the appearance of a self that wills it and has it as "its" desire. (The problem about the subject of this sentence is the problem at the heart of the play itself.) Willing itself eventually begins to seem less a natural habitus than, as Faustus himself at one point unwittingly calls it, a "desperate enterprise." The Faustian project, we might say, becomes a matter of stabilizing the "I" by converting "wanting" in the sense of "lacking" into "wanting" in the sense of "desiring": the formula by which he characteristically aspires is not even "I will" or

From *Two Renaissance Mythmakers: Christopher Marlowe and Ben Jonson,* edited by Alvin Kernan. © 1977 by the English Institute. The Johns Hopkins University Press, 1977.

"I want" but "I'll have . . . I'll have . . . I'll have," so anxious is he to feel himself a containing self rather than merely the voice of a nameless emptiness or an impersonal rush to the void. It is not so much that there are things that he wants as it is that he needs to ensure himself that there will always be some object out there, marking extension in space and time, toward which he will be able to project "his" desire, in terms of which he can experience himself as an interior distance alive in the present and stretching continuous and intact into the future. All his negotiations with Mephastophilis leave the question of wishes to be granted pointedly unspecified and open-ended:

> I charge thee wait upon me whilst I live,
> To do whatever *Faustus* shall commaund.
> (281–82, A text)

> To give me whatsoever I shal aske,
> To tel me whatsoever I demaund.
> (339–40)

> *Thirdly, that Mephastophilis shall do for him,*
> *and bring him whatsoever.*
> (544–45)

And Mephastophilis is in turn reassuring Faustus at the level of his deepest anxieties when he promises that "I wil be thy slave, and waite on thee, / And give thee more than thou hast wit to aske" (486–87). Mephastophilis (besides insinuating that Faustus will get more than he bargained for) is not so much promising him "the unimaginable" as telling him not to worry about not really knowing what he wants, nor about running out of things to ask for, coming to the *end* of desire. Ultimate fulfillment or satiety can be the most fearful prospect of all for a self that suspects it has created itself out of nothing (in order to protect itself from nothingness), and can thus only sustain itself in the "conceited" space between desire and possession:

> CORNELIUS: The spirits tell me they can drie the sea,
> And fetch the treasure of all forraine wrackes,
> I, all the wealth that our forefathers hid
> Within the massie entrailes of the earth.
> Then tell me *Faustus,* what shal we three want?
> FAUSTUS: Nothing *Cornelius,* O this cheares my soule,
> Come shew me some demonstrations magicall.
> (177–83)

It is only with difficulty that an actor's voice, in attempting to express Faustus's enthusiasm, can overcome the resistance of the laconic, inward-turning, brooding tendencies of "Nothing, *Cornelius*," and block out the ominous effect of the pause that follows it. The prospect of wanting (lacking) nothing evokes just for a moment the subliminal dread of wanting (desiring) *nothing*, and perhaps lacking it—as if by a demon in language itself, *that* were what were on the other side (and at the heart) of all imagined desires. Longing and dread are an extremely unstable antithesis in this play. Like the Good and Evil Angels, they are always co-present, inseparable poles of a single impulse (and at times it seems that this impulse as a whole is what is called "the will"). It is hoped that this essay will, among other things, provide a validating frame for Empson's perception of the way in which the difficulty of giving rhetorical emphasis to the negatives in Faustus's penultimate "Ugly hell gape not, come not *Lucifer*" (1507) tends to make the voice that speaks it impatiently, even desperately invoke that which it is attempting to keep at arm's length. Whatever it is that strains against those negatives is also what resists the earlier, impatient *invocations* that the line so pointedly recalls: "Come Mephastophilus, / And bring glad tidings from great *Lucifer:* / Ist not midnight? Come *Mephastophilus, / Veni veni Mephastophile*" (466–69). The same erotic energy charges both utterances, and the later one is the genuine consummation of the earlier one as well as its ironical inversion.

The focus of the play, then, is not so much on a theme as on the field of "terministic" ambiguities in which all its central issues are mutually implicated. An approach needs to be found that can indicate how it is that the play, being about desire, is also, necessarily, about damnation, guilt, self-transcendence, and fear of death; about the body, about self-reference, about cause, motion, place, and duration; about, ultimately, "the whole philosophical mythology concealed in language." Even more than themes and images, we need to look at the *terms* by which the play is organized—and in the process shift the focus of our attention from character-analysis and its attendant ethical judgments to the phenomenological contours of the world of the play and their relationship to those of the consciousness at the center of it. Following the language of inside-outside, or here-there, or now-then, or fast-slow, or motion-rest, through the complications of the text would, I think, put us in closer touch with the intentionality of the play than do the restrictive, morally biased generalizations to which an approach such as "the theme of damnation" seems inevitably to condemn us.

I propose to start with the term "end" and its cognates, and follow it, especially through its interweavings with terms for body, will, and time, into whatever corners of the text it happens to lead. Of all the words in the play, it is probably the one that opens most directly upon central complexities. The language of achieving ends, making an end, coming to an end, etc., is a continual refrain of the opening soliloquy, and it recurs throughout the course of the play ("Now will I make an ende immediately" [513], "*Consummatum est,* this Bill is ended" [515], "Thy fatall time doth drawe to finall ende" [1170]), climaxing in the vacillations of the last soliloquy ("'Twill all be past anone" [1482], "O no end is limited to damned soules" [1488]), and not culminating until the final "authorial" inscription: "*Terminat hora diem, Terminat Author opus.*" And in virtually every instance there is a tension between the speaker's attempt to say one thing, and mean it, and the tendency of the words themselves to generate ambiguity, irony, and paradox. Consider, for instance, "O no end is limited to damned soules." It is possible to take "limited" as an adjective qualifying "end," rather than as an active verb, in which case the focus of the sentence shifts from the doctrinal to the psychological, and we find ourselves on the verge of a purely phenomenological definition of the state of damnation. Even when we do hear "limited to" as a verb, there is a certain resistance to understanding it as "granted" or "allotted" (we normally think of "to limit" as the opposite of "to bestow"); and in the time it takes us to adjust to this meaning, we may hear the grammatically easier and utterly subversive "no particular end is peculiar to damned souls (all men suffer the same fate)." Finally, the awkward, apparently tautological predication of "end" by "limited" can suggest two phenomenologically opposed senses of an ending struggling within Faustus's confrontation with finality—end as extension or as circumference, as an abyss or as the boundary that keeps one from falling into it. In "Now will I make an ende immediately," to take another example, there is a rich paradox potentially involved in the notion of *making* an *end;* a possible equivocation between the volitional and temporal senses of "will"; and a transition from one experience of the time of the present to its opposite effected by the extension of "now" into the five anxious syllables of "immediately" (not unlike the transition from "dying" to dying an "everlasting death"). Or, as a last example, consider "'Twill all be past anone." The phenomenological ambiguities of "past" tend to focus the line on the imaginative process by which the mind experiences time and death, and on the various ways in which it unconsciously preserves, gives substance to what no longer exists: "It will all have finished passing by" (on the model of "til I am past this faire and pleasant greene, / ile walke on foote"), or "It will all be the past, or in the past" (with Homer, Alexander, the Trojan War, the old philosophers, and Faustus's student days in Wittenberg). And there is an irony about transposing into the context of death itself the rather common (but still curious) act of imagining a future in which the present will be past; we are encouraged to contemplate the difficulty the mind has in including itself in the "all" or the "it," and the process by which it contrives to survive its death in the very act of projecting into it. In every instance, the more we attend to implicit ambiguities, the more we find a sceptical, nonjudgmental exploration of human consciousness tending to take the place of either an heroic, dramatistic identification with Faustus or a theological, homiletic disapproval of him.

It is in the opening soliloquy, with its careful delineation of not so much the characteristics as the *symptoms* of a Faustian personality, that the play on "end" and its cognates is most elaborately developed; it seems as a consequence the natural place for this analysis to begin. But before encountering specific instances of the term, something needs to be said about certain peculiarities of the overall texture of the soliloquy. It is virtually a patchwork of different languages: Greek, Latin, bastardized, proverbial Italian, and the "lines, circles, sceanes, letters, and characters" of magic; or, on another axis, the specialized idioms of metaphysics, logic, ethics, medicine, law, and Christian theology. Every one of these languages implies, to a certain degree, its own world and world view: the word "end" will have slightly different connotations depending upon whether you are a Platonist or an Aristotelian, a pagan or a Christian, a Catholic or a Protestant, a metaphysician or a moralist, or a physician or a theologian. But this "Faustian" discourse, which seems capable of translating and absorbing all other languages into itself, seems correlatively to have no point of view of its own, no commitment to any particular world view or governing set of values. And it seems likewise incapable of recognizing difference or distance, or of understanding any other discourse on its own terms. The act of translation (and, less obviously, the resistances of a text) is itself a central motif of the soliloquy, and it is invariably attended by ironies of misattribution or reductive misreading. "*On cai me on*" (A's "*Oncaymaeon*") is, according to one editor, not from Aristotle, but from Gorgias, as cited by Sextus Empiricus; and if it seems implausible that Marlowe's intentions should extend to such minutiae (however appropriate it would be to the ironical tenor of the whole to discover the subversive presence of Sextus's radical scepticism lurking within Faustus's absolutist, transcendental presumptions), it surely is an aspect of the ironical design of the speech that "being and not being" connotes for Faustus not the metaphysical and ontological issues that were the heart of ancient Greek philosophy, but merely the formal, scholastic paradigms by which logical disputation is taught and mastered. *Bene disserere est finis logices* is not even from the *Analytics* to which Faustus has reduced Aristotle's works, but from the *Animadversiones Aristotelicae* of Pietrus Ramus, who "reformed" Aristotle by breaking down the division between logic and rhetoric and devising other shortcuts for mastering him—in both respects symptomatic of the character to whom this soliloquy introduces us. (In *The Massacre at Paris,* Ramus is denounced as a "flat dichotamest," and accused, in words that *Doctor Faustus* pointedly recalls, of "having a smack in all, / Yet didst never [sic] sound anything to the depth." If Faustus would seem to be antithetical in his resolve to "sound the deapth" of all that he professes [32], the condemnation of Ramus nevertheless describes perfectly the shallowness he betrays in the process.) His inability to attend to the full contexts of the biblical passages has become a critical commonplace; it may also be of ironical significance that he quotes (with slight mistakes) from *Jerome's* Bible, thus emphasizing that it is already a translation with which he is involved (and scarcely the translation one would expect a precocious student at Wittenberg to be reading, given Marlowe's anachronistically contemporary dramatization of Faustus), intrigued even here by the presumptuousness of human authorship (underscored by the rhythmic stress on "*Jerome's*"), and haunted as well by its derivative, interpolated nature.

It is interesting to compare, as a means of grasping at least one aspect of Marlowe's elusive critical perspective, the way in which this opening soliloquy reduces every "foreign" language that enters it with the manner in which "*O lente lente curite noctis equi*" (1459) intrudes into the final soliloquy. Here, too, technically, is misquotation: the original is "lente currite, noctis equi." Here too, if you wish, is a flagrant violation of the original context: what in Ovid is a wish to extend a night of erotic pleasure serves for Faustus as an expression of apocalyptic dread. Once again a pagan (or epicurean) sensibility is distorted when it is appropriated by a Christian (or Faustian) one. Yet the difference in effect is complete. The line from Ovid wells up spontaneously from the depths of Faustus's being: it *originates* in him (no time or need for translation here!). Burning his books will not get it out of his system. Beneath its apparent inappropriateness, it is profoundly expressive of the obscure erotic energy involved in his religious passion. And against the feeling that Ovid's guilt-free, flesh-and-blood eroticism is betrayed in this Faustian setting, there is an equal sense that the setting deepens the Ovidian sense by creating a cosmic and spiritual background against which the erotic embrace it celebrates can take on its full, intrinsic value. (Jump comments that the transposition "adds immeasurably to [the words'] power and poignancy.") Faustus's misquotation here seems literally an improvement of the original, in its own language—as if he were further inside the poetry, feeling it more deeply, than Ovid himself. And the haunting, paradoxical inwardness of the line can become even more complex if it happens to remind us that Marlowe himself began his literary career and first achieved notoriety with a translation of the *Elegies*. The contrast between the line's perfunctory Englishing there—"Stay night, and run not thus"—and its spontaneous, originative upwelling (and remembering) at the end of *Faustus* then takes its place as a facet of a complex meditation by Marlowe, implicit throughout the play, on authorship and its consequences—specifically, on his relationship to his protagonist, and on the distance that bringing him into being places between him and his more superficial, complacent Ovidian origins. Certainly no less crucial to the final, lingering effect of the play than Faustus's own passionate breakdown is the accompanying collapse of the authorial perspective, from the ironical, mocking detachment established by the opening soliloquy into the experience of immediacy and emotional identification that the closing soliloquy thrusts upon us. Whatever the actual chronology of Marlowe's plays, no work of art—not even *The Tempest*—communicates more powerfully the *sense* of a "last work" than does *Doctor Faustus*.

When we turn specifically to the motif of "end" and "ending" in the opening soliloquy, what seems crucial about the method of reiteration is a discrepancy between the pointed awareness in the text of the different words that can be translated as "end"—and the correspondingly different senses of "end-ness" that language can suggest—and the speaker's incapacity to respond to the concept in any other than an eschatological, self-alienating sense of "end-point" or "termination." For instance: "disputing well" (already a symptomatically Faustian translation of the potentially less disputatious *bene disserere*) is the "end" (*finis*) of logic in the sense of final cause, abiding concern, reason for being: one is always in the midst of logic, once one *has* achieved its end. Yet Faustus seems instinctively to assume that having "attained" this end means that he has arrived at the end of it, used it up, finished with it—and that as a result there is nothing to do but move on to something new. It is much the same with *ibi desinit philosophus, ibi incipit medicus*. This is what amounts to an ethical statement about the limits of the *field* of philosophy, a reminder that the health of the body and the knowledge of its functions and its orders lie outside the scope of philosophy, yet that philosophical wisdom should involve a respect for the body and the knowledge by which physical well-being is maintained. (And in the context of Marlowe's own "post-Christian" vision, the aphorism acquires a gnomic significance beyond anything Aristotle would have intended: that to go all the way in the realm of philosophy is to arrive at the all-important starting-point of the body, to discover it as the unanalyzable phenomenon toward which every thread of philosophical speculation, no matter what its ostensible subject, ultimately leads us. As if *only* a philosopher could know the true significance of medicine.) But Faustus seems to take it to mean simply that when you are finished with philosophy, then it is time to take up medicine. His experience as a physician has no bearing on his experience as a philosopher, nor vice versa. One art follows directly upon another, each beginning precisely where the last left off, each neatly condensed, predigested, and encapsulated within the covers of its own book.

If Faustus were more at home within the metaphor of "sounding the depths," then the "end" of an art might be a moment of creative fulfillment, an opening upon immanent horizons. But "levelling at the end," which seems so much more obviously expressive of the acquisitive impatience and narrow, projective vision that characterize him throughout the soliloquy, condemns him to traverse only surfaces, and to arrive only at terminations. It seems paradoxically the very nature of his will to go forward, his eyes aiming at a goal posited beyond him, that fates him to find himself always back where he started, empty-handed. As the soliloquy unfolds, the impression of an heroic capacity to originate and conclude ("Settle thy studies *Faustus,* and beginne") gradually yields to that of a more passive, compulsive insertion into the ambiguities of "having commencde." The spectacle of a virtuostic progress through the human sciences is displaced by a growing awareness of static self-imprisonment; the gestures of an insatiable thirst for the profound gradually betray the existence of a grasp that turns everything it touches into "external trash."

Against the emphasis in the first soliloquy on the order of books—on compartmentalization and inventory, on hierarchical ordering, on the programatic acquisition of knowledge—and against the goal-oriented obsession with horizon and transcendence that it reinforces, the shape and texture of the play itself poses an altogether more complicated picture of the structures within which a human life unfolds:

> As are the elements, such are the spheares,
> Mutually folded in each others orbe,
> And *Faustus* all jointly move upon one axletree,
> Whose terminine is tearmd the worlds wide pole.
>
> (667–70)

On the one hand, of course, this is simply Mephastophilis's devilishly laconic recapitulation of the Ptolemaic commonplace: against Faustus's desire for privileged awareness, he reasserts the truth of what has always been and what every schoolboy already knows; against Faustus's submerged longing for a pluralistic universe ("Tel me, are there many heavens above the Moone?" [664]), he insists upon the closed world of classical and medieval order. But the words themselves, excerpted from their immediate context, are descriptive less of a classical world picture than of a field of Pyrrhonist or Montaignian "experience" (or of what a modern sensibility might term a "problematic"): the various spheres of what we experience as the world are not discrete and hierarchically ordered but "mutually folded in each others orbe"; the same is true even of the elements themselves. The very notion of distinct, separable professions, or of explanatory and evaluative sets of finite, static irreducibles (whether it be the four elements, the seven deadly sins, the faculties of psychology, or the entities with which the language of religion populates and fragments the inner life) is an arbitrary imposition upon an "ever moving" field of circulation where everything is made up of and inter-animated by everything else. All revolves upon a single axis, while the concept of end-point and polarity (Good and Evil Angels as well as East and West, North and South) is just a "terministic" reduction of what is really spherical extent. Although any attempt to prove that the play endorses, as well as evokes, this vision of things would ultimately become problematical, one can feel a cherished atmosphere of human kindness and well-being, a sense of grace itself, suddenly descend over the play when Faustus describes to the Duke and his pregnant Duchess a circular movement within which the mind's and language's divisive oppositions and linear sequences are imperturbably accepted and contained:

DUKE: Beleeve me master Doctor, this makes me wonder
    above the rest, that being in the dead time of winter,

and in the month of January, how you shuld come by
these grapes.

FAUSTUS: If it like your grace, the yeere is divided into twoo
circles over the whole worlde, that when it is heere
winter with us, in the contrary circle it is summer with
them, as in *India, Saba,* and farther countries in the
East, and by means of a swift spirit that I have, I had
them brought hither, as ye see, how do you like them
Madame, be they good?

DUTCHESS: Beleeve me Maister doctor, they be the best
grapes that ere I tasted in my life before.

FAUSTUS: I am glad they content you so Madam.

(1245–57)

If one looks at the form of Faustus's fortunes rather than at the frames
in terms of which he consciously experiences himself, one can also discover a "whole worlde" in which all disciplines, all approaches to knowledge, are simultaneously implicated in one another, lead to one another
not sequentially but dialectically. The biblical texts at which Faustus balks
confront him with what would seem strictly a matter of divinity; yet it
is with an ethical sensibility (however impure) that he instinctively responds to it, while both ethical and theological crisis unfold within the
framework of an exercise in elementary syllogistic reasoning. The language of magic, which seems so opaque and autonomous in the opening
soliloquy, borrows heavily from the language of Christianity, and its
invocations turn out to be efficacious (or so at least the devil claims) only
because of the negative significance that theology attributes to them.
Blasphemy, too, turns out not to be self-consummating, but must be
accomplished through a legal contract. The congealing of blood is a resistance to pacts with the supernatural that can be understood either
medically or theologically, as a confirmation of either Augustinian or
Epicurean wisdom—ultimately at stake are two antithetical visions of the
nature of Faustus's damnation. When Lucifer responds to Faustus's desperate cry for salvation with "Christ cannot save thy soule, for he is just"
(714), part of our difficulty in coming to terms with the reply has to do
with the convergence of theological, ethical, and contractual perplexities
on the single word "just."

Nothing that Faustus dismisses in the opening soliloquy really goes
away; whatever he banishes returns as a theme woven into the very fabric
of the play. The result is a curious disjunction between the gestures that

he makes and the fortunes that befall him, between what he undertakes at the level of conscious, rhetorical selfhood and what he undergoes at the level of flesh and blood, "textual" experience. He is strangely out of place in this play that seems at first glance but the logical extension of his personality: if he is the prototype of the "forward wit" condemned by the final chorus, he seems conceived and framed by the "patient judgment" to whom the opening chorus appeals. In the moments when the issue of what is happening to him most concerns Faustus himself, there is always an exasperating feeling of the inability of the mind to make contact with the sphere where its life is taking place, in spite of what would seem the stable locus of the body. This obscure sensation crystallizes in moments such as Faustus's attempt, as he watches his blood congeal, to interpret what it means, and only succeeding when he can manage to *read* it as a text; it is present most obscurely but intensely throughout the final soliloquy.

This disjunction between the organization of Faustus's mind and the shape and rhythm of the experience to which the play submits him (along with the growing conviction that, *contra* Mephastophilis, no amount of the latter will ever "change" the former) is what is at the bottom of the feeling that he is fated, in spite of all his compulsive gestures of bidding farewell and making final ends immediately, to experience it all over and over again ad infinitum—beyond even the twenty-four years of the contract, into the fatal round of the play itself. As the play takes its course, one can sense evolving, through the dialectic between Faustus's forward progress and the depths of the work that Marlowe is shaping around it, a meditation on what is really involved in "settling" and taking stock of a life, and on what is really required in order to "get over and done with, conclude, come to a form, achieve resolution in the self and of the self's works." Against all of Faustus's conclusions and resolutions, Marlowe allows himself only that final, laconic "*Terminat hora diem, Terminat Author opus*"—an ending that, in spite of all *its* ambiguities, rings true with the force of an epitaph.

Especially symptomatic of Faustus's habits of mind in the opening soliloquy is translating "*summum bonum*" as "end," and then bidding the discipline farewell because he has already "attained" that end. The character that emerges here is radically alienated from the very notion of a *summum bonum*. (Faustus is so temporally, eschatologically determined that the language of final ends will come instinctively to mind only in the context of death and whatever lies on the other side of it: "Thy fatall time doth draw to finall ende" [1170].) His undertakings accumulate in the absence of any sense of a highest good—there seems no ultimate rationale for doing or not doing anything (hence the presence of something ominously nihilistic always lurking just at the edges of his aspirations *and* his despair—boredom is to the world of Marlowe what dread is to that of Kierkegaard). Nor can one really imagine Faustus, in spite of his desire to "have" his joys "in full possession" (185), inhabiting any achievement, living and dying *in* any work. He seems able to imagine assimilation, incorporation, and containment only as violent, destructive acts: he characteristically "consumes" his objects, while his passions and enthusiasms correspondingly "ravish" him. Desire and despair generate with equal frequency images of assault upon the body and the boundaries of the self.

Where these prereflective aspects of Faustus's character are concerned, the unstressed, apparently insignificant habits of his language can be especially revealing. When he rejects one of his studies, for instance, as fit only for those who "aim" at nothing but "externall trash" (65), we need not, like him, merely take for granted the pejorative connotations borne by the word "external." The insistence in the language of the play as a whole on a complex, often paradoxical interplay between the inside and the outside worlds (as in Mephastophilis's "for where we are is hell, / And where hell is, there must we ever be" [568–69]), and on the manner in which that interplay is experienced by—or *as*—the subject, should alert us to the ethical and ontological issues that are at stake in Faustus's instinctively negative relationship to the word. The Faustus of the opening soliloquy is initially fascinated by things "external" to him: he values an object to the extent that it does exist out there, as a resistance to be desired, pursued, and taken in. It is only after his objectives have yielded to him, and he has digested them, that he discovers them to be "externall trash." And Marlowe dramatizes the process in a way that suggests that the problem is less with the objectives themselves than with the subjective mechanisms through which Faustus incorporates them. (Part of the "magic" of magic no doubt has to do with its capacity to remain a wholly alien language even in his mastery of it, thus retaining the sense of potency that seems lost to whatever he succeeds in converting into his own substance.) It is as if his inner being were like that of the body politic in *Coriolanus:* all digestive system, without any interior space where the knowledge or experience that enters him could remain in some sense alive and intact. Only by being so incorporated could what is outside the self be experienced as meaningful and sustaining; and—such is the radical dialectic of the play—as long as "external" remains synonymous with "superficial" and instinctively qualifies "trash," then the "internal" will be characterized not by profundity so much as by sterility and emptiness. One of Faustus's rare moments of grace occurs when an uncharacteristic and unpredictable perception of the world in all its mere externality, as apparently no more than a passing diversion, temporarily frees him from his anxiousness to "make haste" to Wittenberg and the end that awaits him there: "Nay, til I am past this faire and pleasant greene, ile walke on foote" (1142). Here a simple, unwilled pleasure in the natural world as something imperturbably out there, wholly manifest and at rest, indifferent to desire and despair alike, becomes the correlative of a leisurely, fertile space within the self where all is well. For once, instead of "aiming at" or "longing to view," Faustus just happens to see. For just a moment the inner life is open upon external circumstance, upon what is given it in the unimaginable present. Vision here seems to originate in the external world, and pass into the subject, instead of remaining the destination at the end of the gaze. And what is seen survives and thrives upon the seeing of it—Faustus intuitively understands that this fair and pleasant green will still be here, just as fair and pleasant, once he is "past" it. The conviction of reality is perhaps stronger here than anywhere else in the play: for just this moment Faustus is allowed to experience not the desire but the *capacity* for experience.

But when Faustus is most "Faustian," he suffers the ironic nonfulfillment of one whose "dominion . . . stretcheth as farre as doth the minde of man" (90–91). Fixed, in spite of all his movement through space and time, at the center of a scene that never really changes, where nothing ever really happens, where his only fellow creatures are the projections of his own inner demons and Mephastophilis, his "*fratris imagine*" (278), he can take sight of the external only through megalomanic or hallucinatory fantasy, and arrive at it only as something that is "gone," "past," or yet to come.

It would be possible to adopt an Augustinian point of view from which to understand this profane, cursed mode of hunger that compels Faustus, and speak of the experience of "sacramental intake" from which he is cut off. But the problem is that Christianity, as it manifests itself in this play, both exacerbates and in turn lives off the self-perpetuating, destructively projective mechanisms of desire in which his "Faustian" appetite originates. The Faustus who begins his incantations with "Now that the gloomy shadow of the earth, / Longing to view *Orions* drisling looke, / Leapes from th' antartike world unto the skie, / And dimmes the welkin with her pitchy breath" (244–47), is essentially the *same* Faustus who cries out from the heart of his Christian despair, "O Ile leape up to my God: who pulles me downe? / See see where Christs blood streames in the firmament" (1462–63). Grace for Faustus would be not a drop of this hallucinatory blood but a cure from the mode of utterance that generates his vision of it. It is in fact only Faustus's rare moments of fully *secular* experience (e.g., the episode with the pregnant Duchess and the dish of ripe grapes) that have a sacramental *feeling* about them. This is the paradox at the heart of the play's vision, and the one upon which the orthodox and the "diabolonian" reading of the play alike founder.

Thus when Faustus ridicules with Mephastophilis "a troupe of bald-pate Friers, / Whose *summum bonum* is in belly-cheare" (870–71), he is both more like them than he knows and less like them than he has wit to ask. For Marlowe's subject is itself a certain Faustian appetite, an insatiability that is finally less a sign of inner capacity than emptiness, a metaphysical lack where one would hope to find a set of abiding, natural appetites. The clown would sell his soul for a well-roasted shoulder of mutton (but not for a raw one), and the pregnant Duchess, longing like Faustus for that which is not, asks in the dead of winter for a dish of ripe grapes. But Faustus, unlike the Duchess, is "swolne with a *selfe* conceit," and wishes to glut the longing of his *heart's* desire; and just what this heart is, or longs for, Faustus himself seems to have not the slightest inkling. Certainly neither the origin of its longings, nor the conditions for their fulfillment, turn out to be as straightforward as those of the belly or the womb—even though the violent onomatopoeia of its language insists upon a relationship to primal, erotically charged experiences of the body's feeling:

> Till swolne with cunning of a selfe conceit,
> . . . .
> And glutted more with learnings golden gifts,
> He surffets on cursed Negromancy.
> (21–26)

> How am I glutted with conceit of this?
> (110)

> One thing, good servant, let me crave of thee
> To glut the longing of my hearts desire.
>   (1348–49)

> Her lips suckes forth my soule, see where it flies.
>   (1360)

The "gluttony" expressed in such passages seems too ontologically puzzling to be come to terms with moralistically. It seems too violently oral
to qualify as the expression of a bodily need. The desire voiced here
sounds like a disincarnate presence inside a body, sensing that for its
fulfillment (or extinction) it requires the incorporation of something into
the body, or some sort of reincorporation by it. The ambivalent feelings
involved are expressed most elaborately in the desperation of the final
soliloquy. There a desire to withdraw into a body is confused with a
desire to escape out of a body; a desire to return to the womb with a
desire to be born from it; a desire to escape death with a desire for self-
extinction. Dismemberment is both feared and longed for, as are de-
vouring and suffocation:

> Mountaines and hilles, come come, and fall on me,
> And hide me from the heavy wrath of God.
> No no, then wil I headlong runne into the earth:
> Earth gape, O no, it will not harbour me:
> You starres that raignd at my nativitie,
> Whose influence hath alotted death and hel,
> Now draw up Faustus like a foggy mist,
> Into the intrailes of yon labring cloude,
> That when you vomite foorth into the ayre,
> My limbes may issue from your smoaky mouthes,
> So that my soule may but ascend to heaven.
>   (1470–80)

Every imagined refuge winds up being experienced in oral terms, and
thus ultimately reinforces the negative feelings about the isolation, de-
structiveness, and imminent dissolution of the self that Faustus is trying
to resolve or escape from by conjuring it up. The earth into which he
will run "headlong" (the reverse-birth fantasy seems very conscious on
Marlowe's part) immediately becomes a gaping mouth, and once a
mouth it will not "harbour" him: the very image of what terrifies him,
he experiences it as both rejecting (it refuses him entrance) and threat-
ening (instead of protectively containing him and concealing him from

the wrath of the father, it wishes to swallow him whole, consume him). He asks to be drawn up into a "labring" cloud, in order to be harbored and to be given birth to as well. But within that cloud are "intrailes": gestation is confused with digestion, the pregnant womb with an over-glutted, sickened stomach. The moment of birth is thus interpreted as a cathartic vomiting, a violently reflexive image of self-disgust and its aggression upon the body that contains and somehow engenders it. Birth itself is experienced in imagery of rejection and disintegration.

The first fantasies that enter Faustus's imagination as he anticipates his magic powers express this "oral-narcissistic dilemma" at the heart of his longings: a plundering of the maternal, enveloping realm ("Ile have them . . . Ransacke the Ocean for orient pearle" [114–15]) is juxtaposed to a defensive walling-in against external threat ("Ile have them wall all *Germany* with brasse, / And make swift *Rhine* circle faire *Wertenberge*" [120–21]). And his apostrophe to Helen develops in accordance with the same underlying compulsions. What begins as a simple gesture of cour-tesy and friendship ("Gentlemen, for that I know your friendship is un-fained, / and Faustus custome is not to denie / the just requests of those that wish him well, / you shall behold that pearlesse dame of *Greece*" [1284–87]), attended by the partly sceptical, partly cautious, partly re-spectful distance that a creator might be expected to take toward the works of his inspiration ("Be silent then, for danger is in words" [1290]), returns, under the pressure of guilt and fear, as a desperate fantasy of ecstatic sexual union—envisioned, again, in oral terms ("Her lips suckes forth my soule" [1360]). This incestuously erotic embrace is then trans-formed, as if by the force of an internal momentum, into a relationship with a benign maternal presence where he will "dwell," and to whom he will return at the end of each day's hazards for comfort, reward, and renewal. Finally, at the climax of the fantasy, Faustus-Helen undergoes a metamorphosis into Semele-Jupiter, with Faustus himself identifying with *both* Jupiter and Semele. His vision thus culminates on the appar-ently inevitable note of conflict, invasion, wounding, violation, con-sumption of the other, an aggressive tearing-open of the womb, and on the correspondingly passive longing for ravishment and self-extinction.

Even when Faustus desires most enthusiastically, we can usually hear a note of desperation in his language. A phrase like "glut the longing," for all its voraciousness, conveys a sense of suffocation and choking: it sticks in the throat, makes swallowing and breathing difficult. Such de-sires are being experienced as impediments, or as threats. One feels that when Faustus "craves" of Mephastophilis to "glut the longing of my hearts desire," he is not asking to be given something out of the fullness of his being, but wishing, more literally, that the desire itself, which is alien to him, living off him, might be extinguished, quenched. This negative orality might be contrasted to Cleopatra's "I have / Immortal longings in me," where the sounds of swallowing open up an interior fullness, and establish effortless yet powerful rhythms of breathing. Cleopatra's longings, even though they are more than her and take her out of and beyond herself, are still *hers,* and they are *in* her, and their unquenchableness is for her an authentic self-affirmation. She generates her desires. Even when she is breathless, she breathes forth power. But Faustus, when he sees hell "gaping" for him, cries out "Adders, and Serpents, let me breathe a while" (1506), imploring those inner, alien monsters that give the self no peace, whose insatiable oral demands consume everything that might nourish or sustain it, even for "a while."

In this context, *summum bonum medicinae sanitas* begins to acquire gnomic resonance. Within the pre-Christian, pre-dualistic ontology that informs Aristotle's ethical vision, *sanitas* can be understood not merely as physical health but, more comprehensively, as regularity, soundness of being, discretion, good sense, etc.—as if (to translate the vision back into the terms of post-Christian experience) what we term psychic or spiritual "sanity" *were* in the final analysis a matter of "our bodies health" (and madness the fear of or for it, or disgust with it, or a fever in it), the state of being grounded and stabilized in the continuity of physical existence. The values implied would seem to be in equal opposition to both Christian and Faustian man—who, from this point of view, seem but two manifestations of a single phenomenon.

C. L. Barber, in a beautiful perception of the way in which the play characteristically works, has noted the counterpoint between Faustus's fearful response to his devils' threats of dismemberment and the clown's contrastingly "sane" reaction to Wagner's threats to "turne al the lice about thee into familiars, and they shall teare thee in peeces":

> Doe you heare sir? you may save that labour, they are too familiar with me already, swowns they are as bolde with my flesh, as if they had payd for my meate and drinke.
>
> (388–91)

Barber stresses the *felt* value of "the clown's independence, and the *detente* of his common man's wit which brings things down to the physical." Yet he seems to back away from the logical implications of his insight when he goes on to suggest that the ultimate effect of the contrast is to "set off the folly of Faustus' elation in the bargain," and to underscore the serious consequences of that bargain: "Mephastophilis, Faustus' familiar, will pay for him meat and drink, and ultimately 'make bold with his flesh.'" In this interpretation, the common man's sanity of the clown is, by a dramatic irony, made to reinforce the intimidating power of the latent psychotic fears to which it seems so affirmatively immune. But surely what it most strikingly sets off is not the folly of Faustus's elation in his bargain but his terror-stricken response to the threats with which both Christian doctrine and its devils intimidate him once he has entered into it. The clown seems more a benign dialectical alternative than merely an ironical foil. (He plays Barnardine to Faustus's Claudio, or Calyphas to Faustus's Tamburlaine.) Here is someone who has lived so long with his personal demons, and become so intimately—so woefully and lice-bittenly—acquainted with them, that he is immune to attempts to threaten him with them as if they were external, alien, persecutory forces—the strategy, it should be noted, of the Christian God as well as of the devil who is his servant *malgré lui* (Wagner's intimidation of this clown is, in fact, a more accurate analogue of one of Christianity's methods of conversion than it is of diabolic temptation—"wel, wilt thou serve me, and Ile make thee go like *Qui mihi discipulus?*" [374–75].) The clown's life of poverty makes the presence of his body, with its needs, demands, and vulnerabilities, the central, inescapable reality of his experience, and thus paradoxically grants him an easy, intimate relationship with the physical that Faustus lacks. Yet the judgment at Faustus's expense, it needs to be emphasized, remains problematical: Marlowe's focus is here as elsewhere less on willfully chosen, self-created personalities than on given, instinctual natures.

Thus when the opening chorus describes Faustus as "swolne with cunning of a selfe conceit," there is beneath the melodramatic surface a morally and ontologically complex situation. "Conceit" can mean either "vanity," or "fancy," "idea," etc. (with only potential, and at any rate less simplistically pejorative connotations of "unreal" or "illusory"), or "engendering," "conception," evoking the image of a physical pregnancy. "Cunning" can mean "craft" or "guile," but it can also be understood in a less negative sense as a sort of ontological potentiality, a knowing that, though neither quite being nor doing, is also a "canning," a "being-able-to." "Swolne" reinforces the metaphor of pregnancy, but (in pointed contrast to the great-bellied Duchess) associates it with a pathological condition—the swollenness of enflamed or diseased parts of the body. "Selfe conceit" can correspondingly be taken as either "vain pride," or

as "self-engendered," or, somewhere in between, as "an idea or imagination or illusion of [a] self"; and, within this third possibility, the idea
of self could be a "conceit" either because it is a false or vain one, or,
more problematically, because the "selfe" is *essentially* a conceit, and perhaps a necessary one. If this conceit is the sickness that inflames and
alienates Faustus, it also seems to be the only thing that offers him the
possibility of peace and rest, the only refuge to which he can entrust
himself in self-relinquishment: "Tush, Christ did call the thiefe upon the
Crosse, / Then rest thee Faustus quiet in conceit. (*Sleepe in his chaire*)"
(1173–74). Even if the moment of grace Faustus experiences here is begot
of nothing but vain fantasy and grounded in sophistry and evasion, the
positive feelings that accompany it are only enhanced by comparison with
the theologically approved version that he is urged to seek, with its en-
joinder to "breake heart, drop bloud, and mingle it with teares" (1306).
Beyond the superficial moral disapproval of the phrase there arises the
potential of a more tragic, poignant Faustus, burdened with his conceit
of self as the Duchess with her child (the last soliloquy his final labor),
attempting to be born, to give birth to himself, to a self where he can
be, and be at rest: having (for whatever reasons) to engender upon himself, through consciousness, what the Robins and Wagners and Emperors
and Horsecoursers of the world are prereflectively rooted in: and thus
fated (or chosen) to confront the ontological void in which ordinary experience is so imperturbably suspended.

Again, it is Shakespeare who offers us a sympathetic rather than a
reductively judgmental contrast. Faustus's closest Shakespearean relative
is Falstaff ("O Hal, I prithee give me leave to breathe a while"). The
latter, derived more intimately (but no less subversively) from the Gluttony of the morality tradition, embodies the needs, the anxieties, and
perhaps ultimately the tragedy of the human self, the embodied self.
(Mistress Quickly knows that Falstaff is *dead* when she lays her hand over
the parts of the continuous, whole object that his body is, and feels that
"all [is] as cold as any stone"; the scholars know that Faustus is burning
in hell—or "gone," as the final chorus more evasively puts it—when they
find his limbs scattered over the floor of his study.) When Falstaff speaks
of his body, it is always with a wry acceptance of it as the locus of his
being; and the result is always to consolidate his connections with a world
in whose otherness he is so elaborately implicated. ("Oversolitariness" is
Faustus's sickness; "company" is Falstaff's ruin, as he himself remarks.)
But Faustus's hunger is radically alienated from the wisdom (and the
tragic knowledge) of the body. So projective both in space and time, it

seems really a hunger *for* a self, for some interior, habitable space where
the outside world as well might appear intact and actual—where real
desires might originate and real responses to them might be received.
When Faustus speaks of (or to) his body—or his soul, or his heart, or
"Faustus"—a sense of inner isolation, dislocation, and abstraction results.
His wording of the contract with Lucifer (it is Faustus who authors it)
provides a telling instance of how unreal and abstractive, yet compulsive,
the act of self-reference is for him:

> *I John Faustus of Wertenberge, Doctor,* by these presents, do give
> *both body and soule* to Lucifer prince of the East, and his minister
> Mephastophilis, and furthermore graunt unto them, that 24.
> yeares being expired, the articles above written inviolate, full
> power to fetch or carry *the said John Faustus body and soule, flesh,*
> *blood, or goods,* into their habitation wheresoever.
> By *me John Faustus.*
>
> (550–57; italics mine)

All this in spite of the fact that Mephastophilis never asks for anything
except Faustus's *soul.* The threat of dismemberment is already latent in
such language. It is as if Faustus, unsure of where to locate himself amidst
the constellation of words that he possesses with which to refer to himself, always elsewhere than where he points, unconsciously wishes to
insure that there is no loophole in the contract that would allow the devil
to claim something that is his yet leave "Faustus himself" behind. (Yet
again, to what does the grammatical subject of my own sentence so
complacently refer?) In the final soliloquy, as Faustus attempts to confront
(and evade) what is going to "become" of him when the clock strikes
twelve, his terms of self-reference begin to whirl desperately about the
blind spot at their center. The stars are asked to draw up "Faustus" like
a foggy mist, but this image of the dissolution of the whole (composite?)
self, named from the outside, is promptly cancelled when it is extended
to involve clouds subsequently belching forth "my limbes" so that "my
soule" may ascend to heaven (1474–80). The body survives its gentle
dissolution, only to be torn violently apart; the "I" continues to speak
and to name its possessions, only to be left behind, abandoned to the
void that remains when "its" body and "its" soul have gone their separate
ways. If it is "my soule" that will be in hell forever (1483), it is "my
incessant paine" that God is asked to end (1485), and this in turn will
involve letting "Faustus" live "a thousand yeeres, a hundred thousand"—
before "at last" being saved (1486–87). When the possibility of the trans-

migration of souls is envisioned, the "I" identifies not with the soul that flies to a new embodiment and identity, but with what remains behind when it is gone: "Ah *Pythagoras metemsucossis* were that true, / This soule should flie from me, and I be changde / Unto some brutish beast" (1491–93). But the beast into which this "I" would be changed is in the process imbued with its own mode of eschatological consciousness: "al beasts are happy," it now turns out, not because they are "wanting soule" (1489), but because "when they die, / Their soules are soone dissolvd in elements" (1493–94). The lines that deny a Pythagorean transmigration of souls thus *enact* the curse of an inverted, Faustian metempsychosis. It is appropriate that Faustus should reject this doctrine by returning to a "mine" that "must live still to be plagde in hel" (1495).

What is it that so doggedly persists in this soliloquy, that resists or actively refuses every image of transmigration, metamorphosis, or dissolution of identity that is seized upon? Amidst all this naming and owning, can one discover a central core of being that Faustus *is*? Where and what is the voice that speaks these lines, that says "Faustus," and what becomes of *it* when the clock strikes twelve? Can the straightforwardness of the final stage direction, "exeunt with *him*" (italics mine), fail to be contaminated by these referential ambiguities and the metaphysical perplexities they generate? Can all our nagging questions about the whereness of Faustus ("—How now sirra, wheres thy maister?—God in heaven knows [206–7]), and all our related difficulties with that phrase "body and soul" ("for is not he *corpus naturale,* and is not that *mobile*" [221–22]), really be put to rest by the spectacle of several stage-hand devils carrying an expired body off Marlowe's stage? In *The Will to Power,* Nietzsche compares our belief in the subject to the error we commit when we say "the lightning flashes," thereby adding to the event (the flash) a transcendent entity (the lightning) that causes or performs the event. If we could imagine this "lightning which flashes" given a language with which to speak of itself (or better yet, imagine the flash of light itself as that language), and then attempting during its span to think in that language about "what will become of me when my flash expires," we might be very close to understanding what it is that Marlowe is attempting to dramatize in this final soliloquy.

Yet certain qualifications become necessary here. For what we have left altogether unaccounted for are the unexpected nuances of Marlowe's own attitude toward this Faustian egotism and the nothingness at the heart of it. The play is always analytical, often ruthlessly ironical, yet Marlowe's distance from his protagonist is never without a strangely benign sense of humor, a bemusement that ranges from exasperation to wry affection. The very aspects of Faustus's personality that should make us remorselessly critical of him so often wind up disarming us instead, perhaps even endearing him to us. When he responds, for instance, to Lucifer's and Belsabub's entrance by prematurely crying out, "O Faustus, they are come to fetch away thy soule" (719), we could describe him as a cowering wretch, and take righteous, moralistic pleasure in this collapse of his facile, stoic-promethean bravura, but in so doing we would miss entirely the gentle laughter that colors his dramatization here. Marlowe's regard for him seems not so far at times from that with which he contemplates the folly of his creatures (and the creatures of his folly) in *Hero and Leander*. There is about Faustus, even at his worst, a certain innocence, a certain childlike guilelessness. Burning with desire to be initiated into the forbidden arts, his instinct is to enhance his plunge into evil by postponing it until after a hearty dinner shared with Valdes and Cornelius: "Then come and dyne with me, and after meate / Weele canvas every quidditie thereof" (196–97). Just after having signed away his soul, and delighted with his newly purchased wantonness and lasciviousness, the best he can do is ask Mephastophilis, to the latter's dismay, for a *wife*. Informed by Mephastophilis that they are going to stay in the Pope's privy chamber while they are in Rome, Faustus replies, again to the exasperation of his companion, "I hope his holinesse will bid us welcome" (847). He responds to the silliness of the pageant of the Seven Deadly Sins with the naive, egocentric delight of a child watching a Punch-and-Judy show. And when he soliloquizes, he seems to be doing the same thing that children do when they talk to themselves, and for essentially the same reasons. Where a less radical humanism would insist upon a central self or a stable core of being, and a more romantic, self-mystified nihilism upon a heart of darkness or a "dumbfoundering abyss," Marlowe's vision perceives, quizzically, a conversational circuit ("Settle thy studies *Faustus,* and beginne . . .")—which, for all the effects it creates of an inner life that is imaginary, ungrounded, discontinuous, and tenuously verbal, still achieves at its happiest an ingratiating mode of self-intimacy ("Now *Faustus,* thou art Conjurer laureate" [276]), and expresses at its most disturbed nothing more damnable than the terror of a child's fear of being left alone in the dark and the despair of a parent's attempt to comfort it ("Then feare not *Faustus,* but be resolute" [257]), "Then rest thee Faustus quiet in conceit" [1174], "Ah Faustus, / Now thou hast but one bare hower to live" [1450–51]). Thus the final soliloquy, a nightmare of self-fragmenting solipsism, a final yielding of the mind to its own hypothetical terrors, yet unexpectedly culminates on a note of pure tenderness, as fear for self turns so far inward that what comes out has the sound of a deep, urgent altruism:

> O it strikes, it strikes, now body turne to ayre,
> Or *Lucifer* wil beare thee quicke to hel:
> > *Thunder and lightning.*
> Oh soule, be changde to little water drops,
> And fal into the *Ocean,* nere be found:
>
> (1500–1504)

One can hear in these lines both the child's fear and the parent's protective affection for it. The word "little" carries with it the same feelings that so often rush in through it to flood the Shakespearean void, as in Lear's "Stay a little," Cleopatra's "yet come a little" and "the little O, the earth," Prospero's "our little life is rounded with a sleep," and, perhaps closest of all to the present context, Hal's "could not all this flesh / Keep in a little life?"

It might help to clarify Marlowe's perspective if we were to think of Faustus as the dialectical, ironical counterpart of Tamburlaine (rather than as a developmental, autobiographical recantation of him), and the two of them together as complementary considerations of a single human problematic. (Their respective deaths might be seen, for instance, as two morally neutral, dialectically opposed, phenomenologically considered ways of responding to the same existentially definitive, yet intrinsically meaningless human event.) The latter asserts that "Wil and Shall best fitteth *Tamburlaine,*" and his tour de force consists of making good on those terms strictly in the declarative mood. To will for him *is* to do— even if the single-mindedness of such a commitment ultimately generates around him the same ontological void that Faustus is always trying to keep at arm's length. The only rationale even for saying "I will" or "I shall" is to ensure that events will be recognized as deeds, extensions of the will, rather than will a response to circumstance or perhaps only a retrospective fiction. He posits his object, then he "cuts a passage" straight through to it. The time is always *now*—yet this presentness is merely the attribute of a vectorial will, not a mode of spontaneous or contingent duration independent of the subject.

"Will" and "shall" are also the words that best fit Faustus ("What doctrine call you this, *Che sera, sera* / What wil be, shall be?" [77–78]), but they ensnare him in the field of human ambiguities to which Tamburlaine remains—perhaps ironically, absurdly—immune. Throughout the play, they shuffle back and forth between their temporal, declarative, interrogative, imperative, fatalistic, and conditional moods, creating for the subject a subjunctive limbo between past and future, volition and contingency, reality and imagination, necessity and (im)possibility:

> GOOD ANGEL: Faustus, repent yet, God wil pitty thee.
> EVILL ANGEL: Thou art a spirite, God cannot pitty thee.
> FAUSTUS: Who buzzeth in mine eares I am a spirite?
> Be I a divel, yet God may pitty me,
> I God wil pitty me, if I repent.
> EVILL ANGEL: I but Faustus never shal repent.
> FAUSTUS: My hearts so hardned I cannot repent.
>
> (641–47)

The words that for Tamburlaine are the cornerstones of the will to power and sovereignty betray, when Faustus utters them, the deeply conditional nature of the self and its compromises with circumstance, situation, other wills, and its own inner tensions. Instead of emphasizing the speaker's capacity to found and enact his own reality, they suggest a sense in which everything that happens to him remains merely possible, imminent, infinitely postponed. Employed by the subject to pronounce its power over time, they reveal that subject instead to *be* an unstable complex of dread, anticipation, reluctance, waiting, remembering, and delay. Even Faustus's most emphatically declarative uses of "will" and "shall" seem fated to arrive in the future conditional. The very existence of a will to something in this play, the very need to say the word "will," implies both a resistance and a reluctance as well as a desire and an intent. Time and again, Faustus will begin a speech on the heroic, self-assured note of "now," attempting to posit (or conjure) the present through force of will; but inevitably its momentum will extend and return upon itself until the moment has been hollowed out into a space of purely virtual, speculative anticipation, whether inhabited in a spirit of longing or dread:

> Now that I have obtaind what I desire,
> Ile live in speculation of this Art,
> Til *Mephastophilis* returne againe.
>
> (357–59)

> Now Faustus must thou needs be damnd,
> And canst thou not be saved?
>
> (438–39)

The "now" in which Faustus discovers himself is thus just as radically circumscribed by eschatological imaginings as the present that Tamburlaine asserts by force of will. What makes it so much more complex and openly problematical is the internal resistance of what has the appearance of a conservative, self-preservative impulse, a preoccupation with containing, dwelling, "living in"—in his study, in Aristotle's works, in all voluptuousness, in speculation, in conceit, in Helen's arms, in hell forever. As fundamentally constituted by teleological, apocalyptic drives as Faustus seems to be, his instinct is nevertheless not so much to fulfill them as to create out of them a habitable, sustaining space for himself and his will—his resolution is to *make* an end immediately. (The ontological status of this "impulse" or "instinct" is crucial for the play's vision of human nature and value: Does it have to do merely with a dread constituted wholly within and in terms of the apocalyptic energies of Faustus's desire, or is it the manifestation of "life instincts" that have a positive, autonomous existence of their own, and thus resist from without his "Faustian" tendencies? How are we to interpret the congealing of his blood?) For Tamburlaine, projects exist straightforwardly to be realized, as perpetual demonstrations of the self; for Faustus, they are "self conceits" that can, at least *until* they come to fruition, be imaginatively inhabited. Where the one thrusts forward, his sword erect, the other reaches out to draw a magic circle round himself.

Nothing, in this respect, could be more characteristic of Faustus and the temporal ambiguities that make him up than to specify of his own accord a twenty-four-year limit to his contract with the devil. To have Mephastophilis wait on him for "as long as he lives" (as Faustus first demands and Mephastophilis himself later proposes), besides leaving a loophole open for the devil, would be to reinforce the sense of life as an open, aimless extension into indefiniteness that he is haunted by in the first place. The feeling of time's contingency, and of the self's accidental, precarious dispersal into it would be intensified—the paradigmatic moment of death would occur when the clock struck not twelve but "one." (It is such a sense of things at which Hamlet seems eventually to arrive: "If it be now, 'tis not to come; if it be not to come, it will be now; if it be not now, yet it will come.") The twenty-four years, on the other hand, become "his" (as, conversely, "the interim" becomes Hamlet's), and at the same time they contain him, concentrate him, *dramatize* him—it is of the essence that they amount to *less* than a normal life span. Contingency and flux are transformed into "thy fatall time," death from one moment among many into "thine houre," the "finall ende" toward which *all* points and rushes.

"Endlessness" is thus a matter of crucial ambivalence for Faustus: if it is the goal that he pursues, it often seems in turn precisely what he is fleeing from. "O no end is limited to damned soules" can be taken as a phenomenological definition of damnation for Faustian consciousness, and not just as an article of faith concerning the nature of existence in hell. The form of the expression makes ends and limitedness feel like things that are bestowed upon you, like grace. ("The *reward* of sinne is death: thats hard.") Without the sense that life ends (terminates) there could be no sense that life has an end (direction, purpose, goal), even if all invented ends then become means for annulling or evading the end upon which they are predicated. Without the imposition of limits, real or imaginary, there could be no striving, straining, aspiring, transgressing, or overreaching—and this would surely be hell for the Faustian sensibility. And, from the opposite direction of whatever it is in Faustus that resists him, only an end given to him as a limit could save him from his own overreaching nature, which, left to itself, would *be* his damnation: "The damned souls *are* those who are deprived the sense of death as a limit, a termination"; or (taking "limited" as an adjective), "The damned souls are those who are unable to respond to any end as limited, terminal, bounding; for whom every goal becomes a means of reaching for infinity or transcending the self; for whom the necessity of dying becomes an issue of living or dying an 'everlasting' death." Again, in hidden tension with the apparently inclusive choice between eternal damnation or salvation is what may be an even more fundamental alternative between mortality and immortality per se (for after all, no end is limited to the souls that are in heaven, either)—as if the Christian soul and the Faustian soul at its most outcast were phenomenologically identical, and both were denied the grace of all that is embodied in a dish of ripe grapes.

The specification of exactly twenty-four years further reinforces this interplay between Faustus's "Faustian" instincts and that in him which holds out for the sanity of a "natural" life. By subliminally drawing upon the paradigm of twenty-four hours, the span reinforces the sense of a human life as something short and urgent, cut off from the larger, enduring rhythms of nature, moving ever further from home and origins, haunted by the linear "passing" of a purely subjective, instrumental time that is yet suffered as something external and daemonically alien to the self ("Oh, it strikes, it strikes"). Yet one can also feel in Faustus's insistence upon twenty-four years a desire to experience himself installed within the natural order of things (compare his initial eagerness to conjure "in some lustie grove" [184]), his life taking its course as if it were a "naturall day" (1457), with time revolving in an endless round about the self at the center of it, containing it, replenishing it, and ultimately returning it to its beginnings (as if minutes, hours, days, weeks, months, years, lives, and the ever-moving spheres of heaven were concentric circles).

It is interesting in this regard that when Faustus's internal time sense unaccountably registers that the end of his twenty-four years is approaching, his instinct is to "make haste to *Wertenberge*" (1138–39), back to the *place* where it all began. It is as if his life were literally coming full circle, and the study in Wittenberg were where his death were going to happen, and he had to hurry in order not to arrive there too late for it. (Again, beneath the fear of death, a fear of being abandoned, left behind.) And while we could take this as symptomatic of Faustus's inability to internalize fully his own death, to take it upon himself as something that happens in him, within the limits of his self—yet there is something very positive about the instinctive conviction it implies that, in spite of Mephastophilis's lessons, life does take place in the external world, and that places do exist apart from and independent of the self that occupies them. (Something similarly affirmative is implicit in Faustus's explanation to the Duke and Duchess that our time encompasses places where we are not, and where things are different, yet where life goes on, as if it were merely a continuation of our own. Time here is not what erodes but what unifies and encompasses, what is held in common ["that when it is heere winter with us, in the contrary circle it is summer with them"], assuring us that the green world is even in the dead of winter present and magically at hand.) The mood of the play becomes for a moment extraordinarily benign. Death is associated with returning home (and fear of death with exile), with a finite life coming full circle. The temporal anxieties out of which life is made do not disappear, but for a moment they are resolved: time still "runne[s]" a "restless course," but it runs it with "calme and silent foote"; Faustus still feels the urge to "make haste," but in that very moment he looks out and sees a "faire and pleasant greene," and decides to "walke on foote" till he is "past" it (1134–42). The world remains at a distance (though for a change, so near at hand!), and the human relationship to it remains one of passing, and passing by; yet for once this relationship seems the source of a deep contentment: the world abides, and Faustus's movement past it is the measure of his freedom within it. Faustus's leisurely walk interacts most beautifully with his apprehension of the calm and silent foot of time. We realize how complex the relationship between subjective and objective experience is: the language suggests a sense in which Faustus is time, and time Faustus. At least the time in which Faustus is caught up and the time that takes place inside of him seem for a moment to share a common rhythm, and through that sharing both gain composure, both are released from Faustian energies that drive them.

Such experiences of grace never amount to anything more than brief, elusive interludes in the play; they remain wholly invisible to Faustus's conscious grasp of himself and his fate, and have no influence at all on the larger, compelling form of his fortunes—one can in fact observe their potential affirmations being systematically converted into terror and despair in the final soliloquy. Marlowe is too self-critically implicated in his protagonist, too intent on pursuing ambiguities and contradictions to their radical conclusions, too insistent on both the fatality and the inexplicable contingency of a human nature, to bestow upon his character a creaturely grace predicated upon an authorial transcendence. Yet these interludes—the fellowship of the Scholars, the walk past the fair and pleasant green, the pregnant Duchess and her dish of ripe grapes, even, in a strange way, the practical jokes at the expense of the Knight and the Horsecourser—are, nevertheless, privileged moments in the deepest sense: they contain the experience that is not only held up for critical reflection and questioned from within but also deeply *valued* for its own sake by the play. It is they, in all their apparent inconsequentiality, that adumbrate the presence of a single, resolved point of view brooding imperturbably, even benignly, over all the play's internal ambiguities and fluctuations. When the Emperor of Germany, given the opportunity to fulfill his heart's desire, cautiously approaches a vision of Alexander's paramour to inspect the mole (or wart) that was rumored to have grown on her neck, and expresses his wonder and naive, self-satisfied delight in actually finding it there, surely we are being invited to cherish—more than through all of Faustus's transcendental projects combined—the sweetness of a human life, precisely *for* its limitedness, for the littleness of its absurd, gently laughable epiphanies. It is, in fact, the background of Faustus's own restless striving, and the religious unhappiness it attracts to itself, that bestow upon what might normally pass as "the trivial" such a deep sense of value. (What pastoral strategy could do for the green world what Faustus's casual, momentary appreciation of it accomplishes?) Conversely, it is the play's drive toward an *acknowledgment* of the Faustian predicament that gives its critical distance and its insistence upon other values the quality of *radical* gestures. And if in the end the play nevertheless remains the "tragicall History" of Doctor Faustus, it is by reference to the touchstone of human happiness and sanity embodied in these moments, and not to one of either heroic overreaching or Christian self-abnegation (the one merely the inverted image of the other), that his tragedy is contemplated and his losses ultimately measured:

> As for the most central of our senses, our inner sense of the interval between desire and possession, which is no other than the sense of duration, that feeling of time which was formerly satisfied by the speed of horses, now finds that the fastest trains are too slow, and we fret with impatience between telegrams. We crave events themselves like food that can never be highly seasoned enough. If every morning there is no great disaster in the world we feel a certain emptiness: "There is nothing in the papers today," we say. We are caught redhanded. We are all poisoned. So I have grounds for saying that there is such a thing as our being intoxicated by energy, just as we are intoxicated by haste, or by size. . . . We are losing that essential peace in the depths of our being, that priceless absence in which the most delicate elements of life are refreshed and comforted, while the inner creature is in some way cleansed of past and future, of present awareness, of obligations pending and expectations lying in wait.
> (Paul Valéry, "Le Bilan de l'Intelligence," trans. Denise Folliot and Jackson Matthews)

Doctor Faustus:
Master of Self-Delusion

Barbara Howard Traister

The ambiguities with which Greene hedged *Friar Bacon* were surely deliberate. When we turn to Marlowe's *Faustus,* ambiguity is again everywhere, but here it seems less purposeful, more accidental. Indeed, the
play presents almost insoluble problems: its date of composition is in
doubt, and it exists in two very different texts, neither of which modern
scholars think to be wholly Marlowe's. These extant texts, confused and
mutilated as they are, have understandably been susceptible to a multitude
of critical interpretations. Yet the very fascination that *Faustus* holds for
critics suggests something of the power that the play retains, even in its
imperfection.

Ambiguity and irony—key words in almost every discussion of
Faustus—are frequently used to explain the play's various dichotomies.
For underlying almost all explication of *Faustus* is a sense that the play's
words and actions do not match: Faustus's rhetoric and his deeds are
incommensurate, and the play's beginning and end frame a number of
prosaic and dull scenes in which Faustus seems totally unlike the scholar
of the play's opening.

Among the reams of *Faustus* criticism are some treatments of Marlowe's use of magic. But most of this work has sought sources for the
magical techniques and terminology Marlowe uses and possible models
for Faustus himself. Very little has been said about the importance of
magic to the play's theme and structure, though the ambiguity and un-

From *Heavenly Necromancers: The Magician in English Renaissance Drama.* © 1984 by
the Curators of the University of Missouri. University of Missouri Press, 1984.

certainty commonly associated with magic make it a particularly appropriate concern for this much-debated play.

In a thorough review of Faustus's magic, Paul Kocher termed it witchcraft and asserted, "Marlowe's play maintains a thoroughly orthodox basis in theology, ethics, and astronomy; it makes no departure from consistency in its witchcraft theory." Kocher is correct, in the main, for as soon as Faustus signs the pact with Mephistophilis he crosses the border that separates magician from witch. From this point on, Faustus does not control but is controlled, as Mephistophilis demonstrates repeatedly.

But Faustus himself does not subscribe to the orthodox theory that Kocher found predominant in Marlowe's play. In the first scenes, he obviously has no intention of becoming a witch or of subjecting himself to any power—godly or demonic—beyond his own. In his expansive imagination, Faustus sees himself controlling spirits:

> Shall I make spirits fetch me what I please,
> Resolve me of all ambiguities,
> Perform what desperate enterprise I will?
> (1.78–80)

Apparently speaking for Faustus and Cornelius as well, Valdes offers an apt metaphor for the relationship that they expect to prevail between themselves and the spirits:

> As Indian Moors obey their Spanish lords,
> So shall the spirits of every element
> Be always serviceable to us three.
> (1.120–22)

Though Faustus may intend to practice magic of dubious moral value, he envisions a straightforward situation in which he will compel spirits to do his will. He intends to be a magician "as cunning as Agrippa was" (1.116). Agrippa rejected magic that subjected man to the devil but accepted magic by which man could compel the devil to do his will. At this point in the play, Faustus—filled with dreams of personal power—would surely make a similar distinction about his intentions with regard to magic.

The path Faustus is attempting to walk is very narrow. Pico's famous *Oration* makes clear what is at stake:

> Magic has two forms: one consists entirely in the operations
> and powers of demons . . . which appears to me to be a dis-

torted and monstrous business; and the other . . . is nothing other than the highest realization of natural philosophy. . . . The disciple of the first tries to conceal his practices because they are shameful and unholy; while cultivation of the second has always been the source of highest glory and renown in the arena of knowledge. No philosopher of merit, eager in the study of the beneficial arts, ever devoted himself to the first. . . . For just as that first form of magic makes man a slave and a pawn of evil powers, so the second form makes him their ruler and lord. That first form cannot lay claim to being either an art or a science; while the second, filled as it is with mysteries, comprehends the most profound contemplation of the deepest secrets of things and, ultimately, the knowledge of the whole of nature.

> (trans. Arturo B. Fallico and Herman Shapiro)

Obviously, Faustus desires the power and knowledge made possible by Pico's second kind of magic; command of such magic would be an appropriate next step from the accomplishments he has already to his credit. Though somewhat self-centered, Faustus's aims for his magic are basically good:

> I'll have them read me strange philosophy
> And tell the secrets of all foreign kings;
> I'll have them wall all Germany with brass
> And make swift Rhine circle fair Wittenberg;
> I'll have them fill the public schools with silk
> Wherewith the students shall be bravely clad.
>
> (1.85–90)

He plans to be a benevolent magician who, like Agrippa, or Greene's Friar Bacon, will command spirits for good, or at least harmless, purposes. His rationale for turning to magic suggests that he expects full control of the spirits with whom he will deal.

Faustus already has a number of the qualifications necessary to practice theurgic magic. He relies on his "wit" to make him an effective magician, after a few lessons in elementary magic techniques from Valdes and Cornelius. Magic is to be the crown of his intellectual achievements, the discipline that will be the real test of his abilities. The two student magicians clearly believe that Faustus will have powers greater than theirs due to his greater intellect: "Faustus, these books, *thy wit,* and our experience / Shall make all nations to canonize us" (1.118–19; my italics).

Cornelius lists requirements for the skilled magician: "He that is grounded in astrology, / Enrich'd with tongues, well seen in minerals, / Hath all the principles magic doth require" (1.137–39). This list is comparable to, though not as extensive as, Giambattista della Porta's requirements for a magician: he must be a philosopher, a physician, an herbalist, know metals and distillation, understand mathematics, especially astrology, and be skillful in optics. "These are the Sciences," Porta concludes, "which Magick takes to her self for servants and helpers; and he that knows not these, is unworthy to be named a Magician." Faustus, with his considerable knowledge, is clearly the sort of person Porta describes.

As sources for Cornelius's enumerated requirements for magic, Kocher suggested a number of contemporary treatises on magic and witchcraft, but he deliberately refused to distinguish between what is necessary for a magician and what for a witch. By failing to distinguish, Kocher lost one of the crucial ironies of the magic scenes. For none of Faustus's reliance on intellectual achievement, proper qualifications, or elaborate incantation is necessary for contact with demons if Faustus merely wishes to make a demonic pact, to become a witch. The concerns he expresses suggest that he is preparing to command spirits, as Agrippa asserted man might do.

But Faustus's preparations are careless and inadequate; he constantly violates the rules set forth by the very treatises Kocher suggested were Marlowe's sources. In his haste to become immediately powerful—a haste characteristic of Faustus, who far too briefly considers and rejects his accomplishments in all major branches of learning—he neglects an important rule of magic, black or white. He resolves to conjure at once, and thus effectively makes impossible the purification, the ritual preparations, recommended by magical handbooks. (Such haste is not present in Marlowe's source, for in *The Damnable Life* Faustus has practiced magic for a long time before he calls up Mephistophilis to be his servant.)

Kocher briefly summarized the handbooks' recommended magical procedures and drew conclusions about their omission from Faustus's preparations:

> The magician cleanses himself by fasting and prayer to God for nine days before the act of magic. When the time for conjuration arrives, he consecrates the circle and all his instruments. If he prays, it is to God, and he never salutes the fiends but wields against them the adverse power of holy names. Theoretically, the wizard is still on the side of the angels. Mar-

lowe casts aside this pretense and makes the ceremony a dedication to Satan from the beginning. He is thus falling in with the classical tradition and with the orthodox Renaissance theological doctrine that any kind of conjuring is a worship of the Devil. No attempt is made to show Faustus as engaged in justifiable operations of white magic.

But is it Marlowe or Faustus who casts aside the ordinary procedures? Faustus's haste guarantees that his conjurations will be futile. There is little hope that he will raise spirits to do his will; his methods suggest that he will fail even before Mephistophilis arrives onstage. Intoxicated by his own rhetoric and his desire for power, Faustus clearly destroys any possibility that his magic will actually work. (Lucifer, of course, is onstage from the beginning of the conjuration scene—he enters at 3.1— watching silently. He has obviously come because he wishes to witness the entrapment of Faustus, and his presence onstage makes it clear that hell and not Faustus is in control and that Faustus's conjuration is unlikely to work as he expects.)

Nothing in the play suggests that Faustus would have succeeded had he been more careful. The play rules out theurgic magic as a possibility for Faustus, although it does not make clear whether such magic is impossible because of Faustus's carelessness or because theurgic magic never succeeds. Had Marlowe intended a direct attack on the possibility of theurgic magic, however, he would more effectively have had Faustus follow all its rules and then fail. As it stands, the play chronicles Faustus's failure, not necessarily the failure of theurgy.

Faustus is blithely oblivious to his mistakes. He conjures; Mephistophilis obediently appears; and, filled with self-congratulation, Faustus asserts his power over the spirit.

> FAUSTUS: I charge thee wait upon me whilst I live,
> To do whatever Faustus shall command.
>
> . . . .
>
> MEPHISTOPHILIS: I am a servant to great Lucifer
> And may not follow thee without his leave;
> No more than he commands must we perform.
> FAUSTUS: Did not he charge thee to appear to me?
> MEPHISTOPHILIS: No, I came hither of mine own accord.
> FAUSTUS: Did not my conjuring speeches raise thee? Speak.
> MEPHISTOPHILIS: That was the cause, but yet *per accidens:*
> For when we hear one rack the name of God,

> Abjure the scriptures and his saviour Christ,
> We fly, in hope to get his glorious soul;
> Nor will we come unless he use such means
> Whereby he is in danger to be damn'd.
>
> (3.38–53)

At this moment, the basis of magic on which the play has apparently been built shifts. Mephistophilis has come voluntarily, not because Faustus compelled him. This is a change from *The Damnable Life*, in which Mephistophilis comes very reluctantly and only after Faustus's repeated commands. Unlike the Faustus of the source, Marlowe's character cannot command spirits by his magic; he is merely a sinner who, by blaspheming against God, attracts the attention of the devil.

Under the circumstances, Faustus sees no hope of obtaining power except by entering into a witch's pact with the devil, and this he immediately proposes to do. He is either so excited by the actual presence of Mephistophilis or so careless about the way he achieves power that he does not mind—or does not notice—that his original assumptions about his control of spirits are being drastically altered. Like his earlier haste to conjure, Faustus's quick offer of a pact is Marlowe's idea; in *The Damnable Life,* Faustus hesitates for some time, trying to find other alternatives to signing away his soul. But Marlowe's Faustus, desperately anxious for the power described by Pico, goes beyond even Agrippa's bounds and subjects himself to the devil. He becomes, although he probably does not realize it, what Pico described as "a slave and pawn of evil powers."

An Elizabethan audience, familiar with witchcraft lore, is likely to have been aware of the radical change in Faustus's position. He is not a magician who, like Friar Bacon, misuses his magical powers but rather a man who has no magical power—much as he desires it—beyond the scraps that the devil permits him in order to mollify him. At the play's opening, Faustus could convince us of his potential to achieve much, whether good or evil, through magic and the power of his intellect. But by the end of scene 3, he has been transformed into a man who so covets power that he is willing to give away his soul for its appearance. Ironically, of course, Faustus not only fails to receive true magic power but also relinquishes the power he already had to govern his own life on earth. He gives himself up almost totally to the guidance of Mephistophilis. The only indication that Faustus realizes the enormity of what he has done comes in a slight shift in his rhetoric. Before meeting Mephistophilis, Faustus continually bragged about his future accomplishments by reiterating "I will." Now he includes Mephistophilis as a necessary part of whatever he may accomplish:

> Had I as many souls as there be stars,
> I'd give them all for Mephistophilis.
> *By him* I'll be great emperor of the world.
> (3.104–6; my italics)

The subsequent encounters between Faustus and Mephistophilis form a pattern. Faustus imagines or wishes for something: magical control of spirits, a wife, knowledge of the universe, a sight-seeing tour of Rome. Mephistophilis replies that what Faustus wants is forbidden or impossible and offers lesser alternatives: a pact with the devil, any paramour Faustus desires, a pageant, practical jokes on the Pope. Faustus accepts the alternatives, usually without argument. The relationship resembles that between a seasoned horse trader and an arrogant but naive novice. Faustus, cheated every time, hardly knows he loses anything, so great is his self-confidence. Only late in the play does Faustus gradually become aware of the importance of what he has given away.

The sense of loss that fills the play comes not so much from Faustus's own realization of loss as from a general failure of action to live up to words and promises. Faustus's aspirations soar above what he is able to accomplish, and Mephistophilis's promises far outstrip what he delivers. Having promised Faustus anything he wants, Mephistophilis cannot bring him a wife, cannot speak of heaven, cannot really do much to enlarge Faustus's knowledge. This sense of failure and limitation, which permeates the final four-fifths of the play, also accompanies, to a degree, the depiction of magical power in other plays. Bacon, Sacrapant, and the Friar in *Bussy D'Ambois* all find magic limited, operable only within certain restraints. In Faustus, however, these restraints are greater, both because Faustus imagines and dreams so grandly and because he is given so little personal power. Through much of the play, in fact, it is not Faustus but Mephistophilis who most resembles the stereotype of the stage magician.

Some deliberate reversals in magical roles early in the play seem to underscore Faustus's essential powerlessness. Functions traditionally the magician's are given in Marlowe's play to Mephistophilis, not to Faustus. Rather than performing in these magical roles, Faustus becomes merely the audience to Mephistophilis's accomplishments.

For example, Mephistophilis assumes the role of promoter of love affairs, as do the magicians in *The Wars of Cyrus* and *John of Bordeaux*. Though finding a sexual companion for Faustus is only a minor job in Mephistophilis's busy schedule, his promises sound very much like those of the magicians:

> I'll cull thee out the fairest courtesans
> And bring them every morning to thy bed;
> She whom thine eye shall like, thy heart shall have.
> Were she as chaste as was Penelope,
> As wise as Saba, or as beautiful
> As was bright Lucifer before his fall.
>
> (5.153–58)

No results of this promise ever materialize, though Mephistophilis does, near the play's end, procure the shade of Helen for Faustus's enjoyment. Despite Helen's beauty, her presence in lieu of a live woman can be seen as another of Mephistophilis's deceptions. Faustus gets the shadow and not the substance, though, by the end of the play, the shadow is his own request.

More visually striking and more significant than magical pimping is Mephistophilis's function as spectacle deviser and presenter. Twice, when Faustus falters and seems in danger of repenting, Mephistophilis produces a show "to delight thy mind / And let thee see what magic can perform" (5.84–85). The first show, designed to divert Faustus from the "*homo fuge*" that appears on his arm, is a dance of devils who present Faustus with "crowns and rich apparel." Faustus is mere audience to this scene, which Mephistophilis creates and directs. Almost all of the magicians previously discussed [in *Heavenly Necromancers*] have created spectacle, just as Mephistophilis does here. None has had shows created for him, however, unless God's spectacles designed to bring magicians to repentance in *A Looking Glass for London and England* and *The Two Merry Milkmaids* can be counted as magical shows. The second pageant, the parade of the Seven Deadly Sins, enters in scene 6 to distract Faustus from Mephistophilis's refusal to tell him who created the world. This pageant is far more elaborate than the dance of devils and reminds us (though it fails to remind Faustus) that all the demonic world can offer is immersion in pleasurable sin. (One of the most interesting verbal details in *Faustus* is the shift in emphasis from power to pleasure as the ostensible object of Faustus's quest. Knowledge and power are continually alluded to in the early scenes; pleasure dominates the middle and especially the final scenes of the play.) Faustus is all that Mephistophilis might ask for in the way of enthusiastic audience for his shows, but he is far from behaving like a magician.

Only after the pleasures of witnessing such spectacles have dulled, after Faustus has seen the firmament, earth, and hell, does he attempt to assume the magician's traditional role as controller of spectacle and magical effects. Having been dissuaded by Mephistophilis from sight-seeing, Faustus finally asks that he be allowed some part in the next spectacle:

> Then in this show let me an actor be,
> That this proud Pope may Faustus' cunning see.
>   (8.75–76)

Mild, polite requests have replaced the commands that Faustus once addressed to Mephistophilis. The spirit permits Faustus to participate— "any villainy thou canst devise, / . . . I'll perform it" (8.87–88)—and from this point on Faustus apparently plans much of the magical action. But the scope of such magic is much reduced. There are no more pageants of allegorical figures or reported trips through the firmament. Rather the magic continually narrows, from shape-changing, stealing the Pope's dinner, and calling historical heroes from the dead, to horning a skeptic and providing grapes for a pregnant duchess. At last, the primary locus of the magic becomes Faustus's own body, as his false head and false leg provide clownish humor.

There is something terrifying in these middle scenes, despite their crude humor. Faustus's magic (or what he *calls* "his" magic) literally tears apart his soul. For the sake of magical jokes his body is pulled apart by clowns, as it will later be torn in pieces by fiends. Once Faustus begins to direct the magic, it deteriorates. His once-glorious imagination is reduced to recalling clichéd magical tricks.

Of the change in Faustus, A. Bartlett Giamatti has remarked: "What Faustus does with his power totally undercuts what we heard Faustus claim for his power. . . . Over the play, the magician metamorphoses himself to a court jester, a fool." Perfectly true, except that Faustus is not a magician. He had hoped to be one, dreaming of himself in a far different role than that of witch. But his magical powers are from the start illusory, though he deludes himself about their nature to the end of his life.

Despite his weaknesses, his errors, and his illusions of grandeur and of magical power, Faustus is worthy of interest and respect as a character. Though he fails to become the demigod he aspires to be, his mistakes are symptomatic of his humanity. Faustus's concern is with temporal, worldly matters rather than with eternity. Accordingly, he responds to sensual experiences rather than to disembodied abstractions: "For the sceptical person the senses are the beginning and the end of human knowledge. Faustus, proceeding in the sceptical manner, doubts the existence of things he cannot directly perceive" (Clifford Davidson). That this is Faustus's method of cognition is demonstrated by his opening soliloquy, in which he measures his knowledge of logic by his victories in debate, his medical knowledge by his cures, and so on. Only the tangible interests Faustus.

This being the case, Marlowe weighted the dice in favor of hell's appeal over heaven's. Critics often remark on the balance of characters representing heaven and hell, good and evil: Good Angel and Bad Angel, good scholars and wicked scholars, Mephistophilis and the Old Man. But this balance is not as perfect as it first seems. The only "heavenly" character to appear onstage is the Good Angel; and not only is he balanced by the Bad Angel, but also Faustus shows no sign that he actually sees either of them. They may be merely external manifestations of his own internal conflict. Hell, on the other hand, has a number of very visible representatives: Mephistophilis, Lucifer, Beelzebub, and many unidentified devils and spirits. Their presence is a constant appeal to the senses; heaven provides almost none (quite rightly, of course, since heaven's business is the spiritual rather than the sensual).

Evil in the play is palpable and flashy. It intrudes into Faustus's temporal world: the devils put on shows for Faustus, parade riches before him, permit him to raise the dead—the tangible proof he had earlier desired of great medical power. All this appeals both to Faustus and to his audience. We understand how Faustus chose allegiance to Lucifer and why; we might have chosen the same way. In contrast to hell, which is constantly defined, described, and even visited by Faustus and Mephistophilis, heaven remains silent and unknown. Mephistophilis will not speak of it; it cannot be visited. Heaven becomes a forbidden, undefined term in the play. Though the deadly sins are revealed and transformed into a comic show that amuses Faustus, the virtues never appear. There is no psychomachia. In the didactic plays discussed [elsewhere]—plays such as A Looking Glass for London and England and The Two Merry Milkmaids—God's power is pitted against that of wicked magic, and heaven displays greater power than evil does. God and Jonah easily outstrip Rasni's magicians, and Justina's resolute chastity foils Cyprian's evil charms. But in Doctor Faustus God does not compete. Even Faustus's punishment is not presented as the active revenge of heaven but rather as hell claiming its own in the face of Faustus's spiritual inertia.

By some few effects, heaven does signal its presence: Faustus's blood congeals; the inscription *homo fuge* appears on his arm; and, in the last moments of the play, an empty throne descends from heaven. In each case, the warning is momentary; the blood soon runs freely again, the inscription disappears, and the throne is simply an emblem of what Faustus has lost. Even as the throne appears in the air, in fact, hell is "discovered," and it probably emits flame and smoke, while heaven's emblem remains inert and empty. These few signs, two of which are so small as to be visible only to Faustus and not to the audience, hardly balance the many visual wonders provided by the devils.

Faustus's repeated preference for what can be seen, and thus for hell's representatives, is evidenced not only by the ease with which he is distracted by Mephistophilis's shows but also by his response to Lucifer's entrance onstage at a moment when Faustus is apparently ready to turn back to God: "O, what art thou that look'st so terribly?" (6.89). The sight of Lucifer erases all thoughts of God. Against the appearance onstage of the demons, heaven remains an abstraction, an unknown whose joys are promised only in some vague eternity in which Faustus never quite believes.

How this worldly and temporally concerned scholar makes and continues in his fatal choice is understandable, though it is clearly mistaken. David Bevington has written, "Paradox is present in *Faustus,* in its moving tragedy of noble character and its explicit denunciation of moral failure, in its hero's sympathetic aspiration and deplorable degeneracy." Marlowe makes clear that Faustus was wrong, that faith and repentance would have been far better than despair and allegiance to the devil. But the careful onstage presentation of heaven and hell makes sympathetic nonetheless Faustus's terrible mistake.

The highly dramatic and eloquent encounters between Faustus and his demonic visitors usually overshadow the scenes of magical adventure that separate Faustus's pact from his death. The most generally accepted explanation of these scenes is that they show the gradual disintegration of Faustus's mind and body as he comes more and more under the domination of Lucifer and Mephistophilis. The different style and tone of the scenes have led many critics to believe they were written in large part by someone other than Marlowe, someone with less talent.

Certainly the magic that appears in these scenes is different from what Faustus envisioned earlier in the play. Though the character of Faustus has been said to portray the contemporary Renaissance magician, unencumbered by traditional literary formulas for magicians, the magic of the central scenes is much like that found in the narrative romances. Faustus's tricks might as well have been performed by Merlin in the course of one of his endless sagas. To fill a large portion of his play, Marlowe chose conventional magic, the sure audience-pleasers, provided by the English Faustbook. This magic distances us from Faustus and sometimes dehumanizes him—as when he is beheaded and delegged—as the romance magicians were often dehumanized. Yet this conventional material has been ordered and shaped to a purpose; the central scenes, awkward though they sometimes are, do more for the play than just represent the passing of twenty-four years.

Faustus had announced his original magical aspirations—to circle Germany with a wall, to stop rivers, to raise tempests, to change the political shape of Europe—when he believed he would be in control, compelling spirits to do his will. None of his ideas was specifically evil or harmful, and several were actually benevolent. This sort of magic, however, the devil is likely to forbid. Just as he can neither describe heaven nor allow Faustus to engage in the sacrament of marriage, Mephistophilis clearly will not permit him any significant magic, nor can he conceivably allow Faustus to perform benevolent magic. To set the Vatican in an uproar, to promote dissension by rescuing the second Pope, to feed the gluttonous desires of a pregnant woman, to raise warlike pagan heroes—these sorts of actions are perfectly all right. But Lucifer will not allow Faustus anything very important or very good. Since Faustus himself is unlikely to wish to do anything particularly evil, what remains is trivial magic that neither seriously helps nor harms anyone.

The process of narrowing the scope of Faustus's desires is gradual. Immediately after the pact is signed, he bombards Mephistophilis with questions about the firmament, philosophy, and the natural world. But, after receiving either no answers or very simplistic ones, Faustus learns to take the easier way, to immerse himself in sensory pleasure, to broach no complicated issues. Mephistophilis is willing to allow Faustus to appear as an ordinary (perhaps even an extraordinary) conjuror who performs standard magical tricks very well, but he allows him no more than this.

Tension arises intermittently in the middle scenes between what Faustus is and what he is believed to be by those around him. Almost all who meet Faustus assume that he is a powerful magician—the Emperor addresses him as "Wonder of men, renown'd magician, / Thrice-learned Faustus" (12.1–2), and Martino calls him "the wonder of the world for magic art" (11.11). In public Faustus puts on an excellent show:

> The doctor stands prepar'd by power of art
> To cast his magic charms, that shall pierce through
> The ebon gates of ever-burning hell
> And hale the stubborn furies from their caves.
>
> (12.19–22)

But in a moment of solitude, Faustus reminds himself of his real position: "What art thou, Faustus, but a man condemn'd to die?" (15.21). An audience that has listened to Faustus's early aspirations can hardly watch him strutting and posturing with his petty tricks without feeling a deep sense of irony. Faustus displays a brave front to the world—even his friends, the scholars, learn only at the last moment the source of Faustus's power—and there are moments when he clearly enjoys the tricks he performs. But underlying all these scenes is his growing fear and despair. The confidence of the outer man, the powerful magician, and the indecisiveness of the inner man, the constrained witch, contrast throughout the latter scenes of the play.

If the cheap magic of the central scenes in some ways trivializes Faustus, he is not the only victim. His audiences—popes, Emperor, Duke—deserve the trivial magic he performs and apparently lack the wit to ask for anything more elevated. The Pope is concerned only for the removal of his rival and for the delicacies that furnish his dinner table. The Pope's silliness is best expressed by the words of the curse he orders:

> Cursed be he that stole his Holiness' meat from the table.
> Maledicat Dominus!
> Cursed be he that struck his Holiness a blow on the face.
>
> (9.101–3)

Similarly, the Emperor's most pressing desire is to see the mole on the neck of Alexander's paramour; having seen it he rejoices, "In this sight thou better pleasest me / Than if I gain'd another monarchy" (12.67–68). All Faustus's clients and victims are frivolous and ridiculous, popes and hostelers equally. Faustus is the *least* trivial person in the play (except perhaps for the Old Man), for he intermittently displays concern for important issues and for human achievement.

The magic of the clowns is, of course, a parody of Faustus's magic and clearly points out its inconsequence. By using Faustus's books and attracting devils onto the stage, Robin, Wagner, and Dick show us again that Faustus's own feat was worth nothing; anyone might have called Mephistophilis. The actual magic of the play, as D. J. Palmer has pointed out, is all on a par—and all worthless:

> Faustus soon discovers the limits of the magical powers offered to him by the devil; they do not extend beyond the natural order. . . . Despite its subject matter, then, the world of *Doctor Faustus* consistently excludes the miraculous.

What is important, however, is the relative worth of the characters who attempt magic, as measured by the attention the devils pay to their summoner once they do arrive. Mephistophilis, who would do anything to get Faustus's "glorious" soul (3.51; 5.73), shrugs off the clowns impatiently. Faustus is important enough to be worth a great deal of time and energy; Robin and Dick are not. Mephistophilis's appearance at the summons of Robin has been used to support arguments for a second author on the basis of a textual contradiction: Mephistophilis specifically tells Faustus that he is not compelled to come by a conjuration; yet he arrives, grumbling, at the call of the clowns (10). But Mephistophilis responds to the clowns' blasphemy as he did to Faustus's. When he discovers whom he has come such a distance to tempt, however, he is disgusted and threatens to turn the clowns into apes and dogs. Robin and Dick have no power over the spirit; he is quite free to revile and punish them. The clowns thus serve as foil to Faustus in two ways: they demonstrate how worthless his magic is by duplicating it, and they suggest how important he is as a human being by the very different response they elicit from the devil. Only Faustus is worthy of serious attention.

One final issue that these central scenes illuminate both practically and thematically is the difficulty of dramatizing magic. Nicholas Brooke has been one of Marlowe's most sympathetic apologists in this regard:

> It is impossible to show Faustus acquiring complete knowledge of the universe, for the obvious reason that Marlowe didn't possess it himself; so he simply states that Faustus did achieve it in two fine choruses and leaves the action to what can be shown, the power of human interference. The result is such a complete lack of balance, that the subject matter of the choruses is often forgotten, and Faustus accused of mere triviality in those scenes.

To this line of argument, Greg objected, "Much more might have been done to show the wonder and uphold the dignity of the quest, and so satisfy the natural expectation of the audience." But the impossibility of staging certain scenes obviously limited Marlowe's creative potential. Much is prevented by the physical limitations of the theater, and much is impossible because of Faustus's desire to know more than any man. But simple dramatic considerations of what would play to an Elizabethan audience must have been responsible for some of Marlowe's decisions about what sort of magic to show onstage. To portray a truly philosophical magician whose only desire is knowledge is not possible; it is far more dramatically effective to watch Faustus's original desire for knowledge and power thwarted and perverted into a desire for pleasure and into cheap juggler's tricks.

For a drama that concerns man's struggle and failure to rise above the limits imposed by his humanity, Marlowe chose his scenes wisely. The poetry, the dreams, and the reported achievements all assure us of Faustus's original vision and allow us to understand why he does not denounce Mephistophilis as a fraud. But the cheap onstage magic forces us to see Faustus's limitations despite the magnificence of his vision. Words alone are insufficient to carry man beyond his station, but words are the only power Faustus possesses.

The power of words, of course, is one of man's greatest assets. Giamatti has suggested the basic analogy between man and the figure of the magician: "Because all men are users of the magic power, language, because all men are performers with words and transformers through words, the Renaissance could figure all men under the single image of the *magus,* the magician." Unfortunately, Faustus's magical powers remain almost wholly rhetorical. He makes his initial impression through magnificent aspirations that impress us for a while. But when the disparity between those words and what Faustus accomplishes is clear, the hollowness of both the magic and the rhetoric is apparent. A major mistake is Faustus's attempt to command spirits solely by words and signs, in contrast to the recommendations of many handbooks on magic that urge, in addition to the ritual preparations, special clothes for the magus, selected perfumes, music, and various pieces of magical equipment as helpful to proper conjurations. But only the language of magic interests Faustus:

> These metaphysics of magicians
> And necromantic books are heavenly;

> Lines, circles, letters, and characters:
> Ay, these are those that Faustus most desires.
>
> (1.48–50)

When Mephistophilis first appears, Faustus gloats, "I see there's virtue in my heavenly words" (3.29). This association of magic primarily with language persists throughout the play; even the clowns attempt magic by garbling words from one of Faustus's books. Dependence on words alone, however, does not work for Faustus; instead of the power he envisioned, his ritual words bring him only devilish temptation and a witch's pact.

Doctor Faustus is sometimes read as a humanist play, a great statement of man's ambition and faith in his human potential. But the play presents a very pessimistic view of man's possibilities. Faustus tries to reach beyond himself and fails miserably. Reluctant to give up his dream, he deludes himself into thinking that the witch's pact will give him the same power he sought as a philosophic magician. Instead of magic that is to grant him endless power and control over spirits, however, he gets enslavement and terror through his contract with the devil plus the crumbs of power with which Mephistophilis pacifies him. But none of the play's other characters has enough wit to achieve anything significant either. Marlowe's play trivializes rather than elevates mankind. Humanistic magic, which appears in the play only as a dream of Faustus, never becomes more than a dream. The demonic enslavement that replaces it in Faustus's mind and soul proves empty and ultimately degrading. The man who desired to become a magician becomes instead a witch and a slave. Magic indeed "ravished" the scholar of Wittenberg.

Faustus's Rhetoric of Aspiration

Johannes H. Birringer

The theatrical presentations of the *Scenes* on which Faustus and Macbeth are going to act out their fatal transgressions quite distinctively create a sense of atmosphere that shapes the audience's perception of the emotions at work in the play-in-performance. Those emotions not only operate in the dramatic universe itself, but also on the spectator-as-participant. In terms of this "structure of feeling" I have said [elsewhere] that the atmospheric effects in *Macbeth* interpenetrate the fragmentary, visual presentation of individual characters. The element of the fantastical, the insubstantial, and the unreal pervade the fabric of the play, and the nature of the human events, actions, and experiences is to be conceived in correspondence with the atmosphere of paradox and unreality.

The collage of swift changes in the presentation of the internal and external events is an important structural device; the inside of Macbeth's mind and the paradoxical quality of its "fantastical imaginings" are dramatized as a kind of nightmare scenery. The competing forces *we* have become aware of through the visual movement of the play flow through Macbeth's dream-consciousness, and the "daggers" in Macbeth's mind reflect the audience's sense of the mystery and the dark processes which so intensely express themselves in the poetic effect of the whole.

The interrelationship between the internal and the external seems far less balanced in *Doctor Faustus*. Faustus confronts us directly and unmistakingly with an elaborate construction of his project and his aspirations. The nature of this construction, however, raises a number of difficult

From *Marlowe's* Dr Faustus *and* Tamburlaine: *Theological and Theatrical Perspectives.* © 1984 by Verlag Peter Lang GmbH.

questions. The exposition of the play, first of all, introduces two Scenes, or planes of dramatic reality; we could call the Prologue's paraphrasing of Faustus's "Icarian" project the "external" Scene of Instruction. The expositor in his conventional role, reminiscent of the older morality form, sufficiently remains on the periphery of the actual theatrical event. The implicit reference to a twofold perspective—the supra-reality of a non-specific, eternal order "out of time" and Faustus's reality as a process "in time"—prefigures the dramatic clash of the external-internal and shapes our anticipation of the paradoxical simultaneity of pre-determination and assumed performatory "freedom."

> *Excelling all,* whose sweete delight disputes
> In heauenly matters of Theologie,
> Till swolne with cunning of a *selfe conceit,*
> His waxen wings did mount aboue his reach,
> And melting *heauens conspirde his ouerthrow.*
> . . . .
> And glutted more with learnings golden gifts,
> *He surffets upon cursed Negromancy.*
> (Prologue 19–23; 25–26; my emphasis)

In a short glimpse, we perceive the contraction and the breaking apart of two planes of time, and we move from the narrative (in the past tense) directly into the theatrical "now" ("And glutted *now*" B 24) where Faustus settles upon his experiment and sees himself making choices. Having been told that Faustus is already fallen, we then see him self-consciously formulate his aspirations and his experiment with himself, and the psychic drama that unfolds in front of our eyes gains a different kind of effect from our ambivalent participation in his flights of imagination.

If we take the Prologue's as well as the Epilogue's assertions of "heauenly power" (Epilogue 1517) to mean that this "power" implicates Faustus's downfall in a universally recognizable "theodrama" or "theatre of God's judgments," we are still faced with the ambiguous invitation to watch the performance of Faustus's "fortunes good or bad" (Prologue 9). How good or bad can Faustus's "fortunes" be if we are meant to trust the Prologue's censorious prediction that the outcome of the play is never really in doubt? Yet the appeal to "patient Iudgements" (Prologue 10) already allows us to ponder how successful the "forme" of Faustus's downfall may in fact be or appear to be if he—as we are to find out shortly—can manage actually to practice "more than heauenly power permits" (Epilogue 1517). The Prologue's critical outline is a tantalizing one because it ultimately introduces the very complex problem of Faustus's dream of *freedom,* and the question whether this dream collapses in or holds out against the ultimate acceptance of the limited role of the self-as-performer in God's Theatre cannot be as conveniently answered as the Prologue's paradigmatic outline suggests.

Marlowe creates considerable tension precisely by setting up the Prologue's critical summary in immediate contrast to Faustus's dramatic justification of his claims; the question whether they are good or bad is only answerable in the context in which they are now performed. Audience response begins to be manipulated in the very moment in which its involvement becomes stronger than the warning voice of the Prologue. And in view of the intensity of Faustus's soliloquizing and his absolute visual centrality on stage, the extent to which an audience becomes involved certainly depends on the effect created by Faustus's (the actor's) very immediate entry into the realm of argument, fantasy, and forbidden desire—a mixture which is explosive precisely because the moralizing Prologue has already denounced it beforehand.

Faustus's dream of freedom and transcendence is behind almost everything he says in the very beginning. "Word" and "act" articulate a sweeping revision of the prior instruction of the Prologue, and Faustus's speech of self-definition contains in itself the philosophical frame of the whole tragedy. Similar to Marlowe's other plays, reality in *Doctor Faustus* is constituted and presented largely through the rhetorical *tours de force* of the protagonist (cf. Tamburlaine, Barabas, the Guise, Mortimer). Together with his astonishing stage-craft, Marlowe's control over language seems to have been magnificently conducive to the intellectual fantasies of his poetic drama.

With a swift, disruptive vigour, Faustus leaps from his implicit *appetite* ("swolne with cunning"; "glutted") through his *self-conceits* to the all-consuming project ("his chiefest blisse" Prologue 28). The leap, as a means of asserting his freedom, is necessary and fundamental, and it is animated by the rhetorical style with which he voices his desires. In the centre of the Faustian ethos we therefore discover not only an intellectual concept but also a concept of the power of language, a Faustian poetics, so to speak, which corresponds to the implications of his breaking away from normative boundaries. Unlike Macbeth's half-realized, subconscious hopes and fears, Faustus's aspirations are fully and explicitly expressed; they are rendered desirable by the self-intoxicating power of the language Faustus uses.

What are the characteristics of Faustus's rhetoric of aspiration? And how are the rhetorical features related to the nature of his project? The poetic texture of Faustus's speeches exposes the precarious balance that is achieved by the heavily rhetorical quality of his "conceits." Faustus has to transform the stage into a platform for his overreaching project, and the imaginative level of his desires is transported to us by the power of *persuasion* through which Faustus can sustain the prospects for the future in the conceited space between desire and fulfilment. Rhetoric as persuasion thus forms one of the central stratagems in the organization of the argument. (Traditionally, persuasion has been regarded as the primary goal of rhetoric, and all rhetorical training was directed at the acquisition of oratorical skills. I am here concerned with the distinctive function of verbal organization and ornamentation in the dramatic context and in their relation to the thematic focus. Marlowe's educational background certainly exposed him to an extensive familiarity with the methods of rhetorical [oral] expression and its comprehensive applicability to all forms of writing in verse or prose.)

> Settle thy studies Faustus, and beginne
> To sound the deapth of that thou wilt professe
> . . . .
> Yet leuell at the end of euery Art,
> And liue and die.
>
> (A 1–2; 4–5)

The ambivalence of Faustus's rhetoric, its inner- and outer-directed appeals, is further complicated by the emotiveness and intensity of the Marlovian hero's all-or-nothing attitude, which characteristically propels the language of the play into the foreground; rhetorical modes often dominate the events on stage, and it is through Faustus's language that we must try to understand what he creates about himself inside his mind. This immediately opens the question whether we see "through" Faustus's pervasive rhetoricity into his mind—as we do in Macbeth's case—or whether we in fact cannot resist complicity with the powers of poetry that kindle our own imagination.

If we take Faustus's initial remark ("be a Diuine *in shew*" A 33; my emphasis) at face value, we are advised to pay attention, first of all, to the style and the function of language in the presentation of the protagonist. The energies of Faustus's idiom are complex enough to challenge a primary, rhetorical criticism that can stay clear of the interpretive problems which are bound to arise if one approaches the play either from a "romantic" or from an orthodox-moralizing point of view.

Marlowe, well versed in the tradition of rhetoric, had already shown a particular interest in Ovid when he translated the *Elegies*. I quote from the second book:

> Verses reduce the horned bloody moon,
> And call the sun's white horses back at noon.
> Snakes leap by verse from caves of broken mountains,
> And turned streams run backward to their fountains.
> Verses ope doors; and locks put in the post,
> Although of oak, to yield to verses boast.
>
> (2.1.23–28)

The spell-binding force of rhetorical and poetical "charms" (the English word "charm," with its connotations of "magic" and "power," is derived from the Latin *carmen*—the word Marlowe correctly translates as "verse" or "song") and the momentum and violence that poetry can have (its power to "break" things apart) signal the essential function which becomes integrated in Faustus's poetic metamorphosis of his dream of freedom.

When we speak about magic or dream or power, we of course speak about a mode or style of self-expression and self-presentation which presupposes a certain attitude towards reality, "dramatic" or "real," that cannot readily be defined by the categories of the serious or "merely" rhetorical. Within the fictional worlds of poetry—and Marlowe's interest in Ovid's *Metamorphoses* and *Amores* speaks for itself—rhetorical style can very well have its own dynamic premises, and before we judge the kind of self Faustus poses in his opening soliloquy, we ought to be aware of the uneasy intersections between the contexts of rhetoric and action and the primary importance of style to which "reality" must yield.

The style of language or language-behaviour answers the questions about the dramatic *persona* who en-acts and lives his role and presents himself in some kind of dynamic relationship with those boundary conditions that normally restrict man. In Faustus's opening speech we hear a great deal about boundaries and limitations, and if we listen to the tone and the content of what he says, our first impression of Faustus's mighty line need not ground itself in any traditional ethical dimension at all. It lies in the very nature of the kind of drama Marlowe wrote that we understand the rhetorical impetus of Faustus's speech as, first of all, a dynamic assertion of his will and his individual voice.

This sense of confidence and upward-moving desire is again quite beautifully expressed in another boisterous revision of Ovid's elegy on poetry:

> [*vivam, pasque mei multa superstes erit*]
> I'll live, and as he pulls me down mount higher.
> (1.15.42)

It is this "leaping in poetry" that we encounter in the Faustian rhetoric. In the line from the *Elegies,* Marlowe deliberately employs the language of paradox, and the second part of the line, with its striking antithesis and its spirited assertion of immortality (we should also note the "over-flow" in the extrametrical line), alerts us to the range of possibilities in the complex interplay of rhetorical figures and tonal qualities, and to the vigour and ease of the metrics and the many effects of ambiguity, irony, and paradox that can be evoked by poetic images.

We see, for example, how in the "snakes leap by verse" passage the central metaphor (the "transcending," breaking power of verse) is expanded into separate metaphors (*distributio*), variation on the theme, repetition (*anaphora; epizeuxis*), and then elaborated by the joining of tropes which tilt the meaning towards paradox and its often grotesque meanings ("horned bloody moon"; "the sun's white horses"; "leaping snakes"; "broken mountains"; "turned streams"; "verse" opening "doors"; etc.).

The expression "verses boast" hints at another major rhetorical figure which Marlowe uses throughout: amplification. It is clear from the conception of his overreaching hero that *hyperbole,* the trope of excess or of the "over-throw," forms an essential, necessary precondition for a project like Faustus's, because it is a mode of speech *and* thought, relating language to ethos, which sublimates the self's exultation in its own operations. From the very beginning, Faustus's speech shows a state of mind to which the desire to transcend appears as an imperative: limitations exist to be overcome. This insatiability had already been imaged by the Prologue's allusions to Faustus's "appetite," and those images were of course entirely negative. When Faustus begins to "professe" himself, the images of hunger and gluttony become much more ambivalent and puzzling (natural appetite/metaphysical longing; fullness/emptiness; learning/cunning; beginning/end).

Again, like the Ovidian "verses boast," the coupling of positive and negative connotations or ironic qualifications ("profites in Diuinitie"; "fruitfull plot"; "diuelish exercise"; "sweete magicke"; "chiefest blisse") creates a sense of disparity which progresses into the central Faustian rhetoric of paradox on which many of the play's symbolic disjunctions rest (external/internal; Heaven/Hell; reality/magic; infinity/human contingency). Faustus himself rushes out to confirm his paradoxical satiety, his longing, and his lack:

> How am I *glutted* with *conceit* of *this*?
> Shall I make spirits fetch me what I please,
> Resolue me of all ambiguities,
> Performe what desperate enterprise I will?
>   (A 110–13; my emphasis)

What is his "conceit"? If we look at the soliloquy as a whole and examine its rhetorical divisions, we recognize the density of its verbal composition and the interrelationship of its individual figures and metaphors. In fact, the entire staging of Faustus's opening soliloquy—in the visual and verbal enactment of his own conception of himself—could be called hyperbolical. He ventures to break down all limits, all conventions, all restrictions. After the initial *apostrophe* ("Settle thy studies Faustus, and beginne / To sound the deapth of that thou wilt professe"), the soliloquy falls structurally into two parts (the review of the human sciences; the exposition of his magical enterprise); yet rhetorically one can see a rising curve of amplification. He is "heaping up" his unconscious desires before he leaps into the unrestricted realm of imagination and the Sublime.

The explosive energy of the strain of paradox is contained in various phases of distribution, division, accumulation, and progression, and culminates in the last lines of the soliloquy:

> O what a world of profit and delight,
> Of power, of honor, of omnipotence
> Is promised to the studious Artizan?
> All things that mooue betweene the quiet poles
> Shalbe at my commaund, Emperours and Kings,
> Are but obeyd in their seuerall prouinces:
> Nor can they raise the winde, or rend the cloudes:
> But his dominion that exceedes in this,
> Stretcheth as farre as doth the minde of man.
> A sound Magician is a mighty god:
> Heere Faustus trie thy braines to gaine a deitie.
>   (A 83–93)

This is the powerful climax of a puzzling stage performance. Before he actually reaches this point, he seems to be involved in what one might want to call a piece of histrionic "extravaganza." With a lot of cunning and nerve, he energetically and impatiently hurries through his review of the human sciences, or at least those that he chooses to attack. His discourse shows a good sense of timing, and his argumentation, his overtly ingenious glossing and qualifying, his multilingual disputation and his impressive verbal and theatrical performance (his browsing through the books is accompanied by a great number of short exclamations, gestures, rhetorical questions, aphorisms, clever puns, witty sneers, and self-conscious assertions) make his lecture seem highly coherent and compelling. Commentators usually tend to overemphasize the ironic undertones and the hidden contradictions in the speech; in its theatrical immediacy, I should think, the Faustian rhetoric can quite successfully mobilize our imaginations and shelter the process of mystification that goes into his "role-taking."

The heroic promise in the hero's conceit and his emphatic visual centrality (he dominates centre-stage throughout the first 160 lines) help to magnify the attraction and curiosity that pull us toward him. Two further presentational devices seem noteworthy; first, Faustus intensively turns to the *objects* of his concern and his ravishment: his books. The references to certain passages and texts are theatrically underlined by his treatment of the prop. Surveying his books, Faustus will pick them up, open them, express dissatisfaction, and finally displace them by his quest for the nonreferential, abstract, and transcending "end" of desire. "Levelling at the end," striving for a goal and generating a final purpose, indicates a leitmotif that attains crucial significance in view of his "finalizing" act of trespassing (the pact with Lucifer).

Secondly, we should stress the visual immediacy of Faustus's self-presentation and his relentless enactment of what he creates as his identity. There is no gradual integration into the plot, as in *Macbeth,* but an emphatic eagerness and disposition to plunge right into the centre. The movement and urgency in his acting style create the impression of an onward surge, and this effect is reinforced and sustained by the poetry he speaks, by the progressive intensity of expression within the line or the verse paragraph. The association of technique with meaning becomes obvious in the very manner in which the speech builds up rhythmically towards the point when Faustus discloses his true objective and exclaims:

> These Metaphisickes of Magicians,
> And Negromantike books are heauenly.
> (A 79–80)

Our perception of the protagonist's character is indeed formed by his use of language. His rhetoric conveys an impressive ability to originate and conclude ("settle"; "beginne"; "end"), and it seems as if he is drawing the borderlines of human knowledge ("euery art"; "chiefest end"; "*Summum bonum*"). His discourse is permeated by figures of amplification (superlatives, comparatives), by exclamation and rhetorical questions. There is a constant interplay of antithetical positions and an emphasis on the repetition of key-words ("end"; "nothing"; "but"; "all"; "every"), and the dominant pattern in the progression of the speech is the symmetry of question and answer, thesis and antithesis. It is quite possible that this accent on dichotomies and the rhetorical bent of this kind of dialectic are based on the teaching of Petrus Ramus who had devised new methods for the construction of arguments and formulated a number of highly interesting *axiomata* for the art of discourse.

Furthermore, Faustus often begins a section with a series of rhetorical questions *(pysma)* which he answers himself *(subiectio)*, falling into his typical, provocative overstatements that implicitly intensify the underlying tenor of paradox.

> Affoords this Art no greater myracle?
> Then reade no more, thou hast attaind the end
> . . . .
> Are not thy billes hung vp as monuments,
> Whereby whole Citties haue escapt the plague,
> And thousand desprate maladies beene easde?
> Yet art thou still but Faustus, and a man.
>
> (A 39–40; 50–53)

Faustus confronts himself with the problem of mortality and finitude; the rhetorical progression moves from the external objects (the books from which he quotes) to the particular and defined worlds or orders they represent. Paraphrasing their individual idioms, Faustus concocts a discourse that translates and assimilates all other languages (Greek, Latin, Italian, English, and the jargons of the individual fields) into itself. His scornful review of the limited and limiting fields makes him arrive at "end-points," he moves from the outside to the inside, questioning his own status and capabilities. The terminations he arrives at paradoxically confirm his will to go forward, to transcend the limits. Of course he does not see the curious illogicality in some of his propositions. In his conscious rhetorical selfhood he seems simply to negate the limits of the generally accepted normative order which defines his human nature (his mortal body, his thinking), and he proceeds to redefine his own *summum bonum*.

His dream of freedom from limits explodes in his fantasies, and the speech in which he anticipates his magic power ("O what a world of profit and delight") is certainly the hyperbolical speech *par excellence*. As soon as Faustus steps outside the orthodox realm of normative tradition, outside his social and intellectual environment, his explicit formulations of his ambitions indeed convey an aura of "opening up." The speech becomes expansive, grandiose, soaring; its imaginative force opens upon abstract horizons. It is here that one feels Faustus's vision unfolding free from limits; it stretches itself and has that upward thrust ("mooue"; "raise"; "exceed"; "stretcheth as farre") which is so significant for the whole idea of leaping.

On the one hand, the rhetoric of paradox seems to enforce this poetic *fusion* of his self with his fiction. The paradoxical interplay ("Metaphisickes of Magicians"; "heauenly Negromantike books"; "Magician-god") transports the Faustian vision onto another level; the contradictions overlap, burst, and set free. Faustus uses the language of paradox and daringly treats magic as if it was freedom, a means of transcendence, a private eschatology.

On the other hand, one can at least anticipate the tragic ironies within the act of liberation. The burst of freedom in its paradoxical nature contains an immanent fission at the same time. The disparate elements in the rhetoric can fall apart, regressively destroy the leap and restrict again. This is most likely to become visible in the relation between the vocabulary itself and Faustus's claim to freedom. His rhetoric frees him and restricts him at the same time. Throughout the play we become increasingly aware of this double effect of liberation and restriction. During his first assertion of his dream of power (A 79–93) it already becomes obvious that he is searching for "new" words, a "new" language; yet the "Negromantike books" he refers to will in turn establish their own limiting system of "lines, circles, sceanes, letters and characters" (A 81).

The language of magic that is supposed to set him free in fact merely constitutes another form of imprisonment and, ironically enough, borrows extensively from the idiom of Christianity. The greatest problem for Faustus is that he has yet to find out what his *summum bonum* really is or might be. In the "sage conference" (A 131) with his friends Valdes and Cornelius he is still trying to redefine his "ends" (cf. A 110–29). We already gain a feeling that Faustus's rhetoric of paradox cannot veil the discrepancy between his subjective "leaps" on the one hand, and his incapability of recurring to another code of language, on the other hand, which might indeed correspond to his dream of freedom.

This predicament, of course, lies at the heart of his tragic downfall. . . . The complicated relationship between Faustus's rhetoric of paradox and the dramatic conventions of self-condemnation which Marlowe enforces throughout is introduced and sustained in a manner which draws attention to the *style* of Faustus's transgression and not, as it is often argued, to the traditional, ethical context against which he defines his role. Christian metaphysics and ethics are referred to as an anti-background, so to speak; and this anti-background is brought into play by the energies Faustus sets free rhetorically. Whereas Macbeth recognizes his transgression—even before he has actually done the deed—as "horrible imaginings," as a bottomless dream which enmeshes him in the catastrophic consequences of an almost involuntary compulsion, Faustus celebrates his rebellious dreams of power and "heauenly" magic.

Faustus possesses the symbolic force of the will which can render him an archetype of a whole culture, or a spiritual attitude, and this force largely rests on the pervasive theme of man's desire to mount beyond natural limitation. As I suggested, Faustus's flights of imagination present a self that trusts its own power over language and, instead of allowing us to understand the precarious working of the mind, bedazzles itself and the audience with its hyperbolic mannerisms. Yet this mode of self-presentation is important for our perception of the play; unlike Tamburlaine, Faustus has no direct opponents and followers who would listen to him. He is alone with himself, and the battle is waged with the verbal, metaphysical, and psychological limitations which his very rhetoric purports to deny.

Doctor Faustus (ca. 1589–92): Subversion through Transgression

Jonathan Dollimore

One problem in particular has exercised critics of *Doctor Faustus:* its structure, inherited from the morality form, apparently negates what the play
experientially affirms—the heroic aspiration of "Renaissance man." Behind this discrepancy some have discerned a tension between, on the one
hand, the moral and theological imperatives of a severe Christian orthodoxy and, on the other, an affirmation of Faustus as "the epitome of
Renaissance aspiration . . . all the divine discontent, the unwearied and
unsatisfied striving after knowledge that marked the age in which Marlowe wrote" (*Doctor Faustus,* ed. Roma Gill).

Critical opinion has tended to see the tension resolved one way or
another—that is, to read the play as ultimately vindicating either Faustus
or the morality structure. But such resolution is what *Doctor Faustus* as
interrogative text resists. It seems always to represent paradox—religious
and tragic—as insecurely and provocatively ambiguous or, worse, as
openly contradictory. Not surprisingly Max Bluestone, after surveying
some eighty recent studies of *Doctor Faustus,* as well as the play itself,
remains unconvinced of their more or less equally divided attempts to
find in it an orthodox or heterodox principle of resolution. On the contrary: "Conflict and contradiction inhere everywhere in the world of this
play." If this is correct then we might see it as an integral aspect of what
Doctor Faustus is best understood as: not an affirmation of Divine Law,
or conversely of Renaissance Man, but an exploration of subversion
through transgression.

From *Radical Tragedy: Religion, Ideology and Power in the Drama of Shakespeare and His
Contemporaries.* © 1984 by Jonathan Dollimore. University of Chicago Press, 1984.

Limit and Transgression

Raymond Williams has observed how, in Victorian literature, individuals encounter limits of crucially different kinds. In *Felix Holt* there is the discovery of limits which, in the terms of the novel, are enabling: they vindicate a conservative identification of what it is to be human. In complete contrast *Jude the Obscure* shows its protagonist destroyed in the process—and ultimately because—of encountering limits. This is offered not as punishment for hubris but as "profoundly subversive of the limiting structure" ("Forms of English Fiction in 1848"). *Doctor Faustus*, I want to argue, falls into this second category: a discovery of limits which ostensibly forecloses subversive questioning in fact provokes it.

What Erasmus had said many years before against Luther indicates the parameters of *Doctor Faustus*'s limiting structure:

> Suppose for a moment that it were true in a certain sense, as Augustine says somewhere, that "God works in us good and evil, and rewards his own good works in us, and punishes his evil works in us." . . . Who will be able to bring himself to love God with all his heart when He created hell seething with eternal torments in order to punish His own misdeeds in His victims as though He took delight in human torments?
> (*Renaissance Views of Man*, ed. S. Davies)

But Faustus is not *identified* independently of this limiting structure and any attempt to interpret the play as Renaissance man breaking out of medieval chains always founders on this point: Faustus is constituted by the very limiting structure which he transgresses and his transgression is both despite and because of that fact.

Faustus is situated at the centre of a violently divided universe. To the extent that conflict and contradiction are represented as actually of its essence, it appears to be Manichean; thus Faustus asks, "Where is the place that men call hell?" and Mephostophilis replies, "Within the bowels of these elements," adding:

> when all the world dissolves
> And every creature shall be purify'd,
> All places shall be hell that is not heaven.
> (5.117, 120, 125–27)

If Greg is correct, and "purified" means "no longer mixed, but of one essence, either wholly good or wholly evil" (*Marlowe's Doctor Faustus,* Parallel Texts), then the division suggested is indeed Manichean. But more important than the question of precise origins is the fact that not only heaven and hell but God and Lucifer, the Good Angel and the Bad Angel, are polar opposites whose axes pass through and constitute human consciousness. Somewhat similarly, for Mephostophilis hell is not a place but a state of consciousness:

> Hell hath no limits, nor is circumscrib'd
> In one self place, but where we are is hell,
> And where hell is, there must we ever be.
> (5.122–24)

From Faustus's point of view—one never free-ranging but always coterminous with his position—God and Lucifer seem equally responsible in his final destruction, two supreme agents of power deeply antagonistic to each other yet temporarily cooperating in his demise. Faustus is indeed their subject, the site of their power struggle. For his part God is possessed of tyrannical power—"heavy wrath" (1.71 and 19.153), while at the beginning of scene 19 Lucifer, Beelzebub and Mephostophilis enter syndicate-like "to view the *subjects* of our monarchy." Earlier Faustus had asked why Lucifer wanted his soul; it will, replies Mephostophilis, "enlarge his kingdom" (5.40). In Faustus's final soliloquy both God and Lucifer are spatially located as the opposites which, *between them,* destroy him:

> O, I'll leap up to my God! Who pulls me down?
>
> see where God
> Stretcheth out his arm and bends his ireful brows
>
> My God, my God! Look not so fierce on me!
>
> Ugly hell, gape not! Come not, Lucifer.
> (ll. 145, 150–51, 187, 189)

Before this the representatives of God and Lucifer have bombarded Faustus with conflicting accounts of his identity, position and destiny. Again, the question of whether in principle Faustus can repent, what is the point of no return, is less important than the fact that he is located on the axes of contradictions which cripple and finally destroy him.

By contrast, when, in Marlowe's earlier play, Tamburlaine speaks of the "four elements / Warring within our breasts for regiment" he is speaking of a dynamic conflict conducive to the will to power—one which "doth teach us all to have aspiring minds" (1.2.7)—not the stultifying contradiction which constitutes Faustus and his universe. On this point alone *Tamburlaine* presents a fascinating contrast with *Doctor Faustus*. With his indomitable will to power and warrior prowess, Tamburlaine really does approximate to the self-determining hero bent on transcendent autonomy—a kind of fantasy on Pico's theme of aspiring man. But like all fantasies this one excites as much by what it excludes as what it exaggerates. Indeed exclusion may be the basis not just of Tamburlaine as fantasy projection but *Tamburlaine* as transgressive text: it liberates from its Christian and ethical framework the humanist conception of man as essentially free, dynamic and aspiring; more contentiously, this conception of man is not only liberated from a Christian framework but reestablished in open defiance of it. But however interpreted, the objective of Tamburlaine's aspiration is very different from Pico's; the secular power in which Tamburlaine revels is part of what Pico wants to transcend in the name of a more ultimate and legitimate power. Tamburlaine defies origin, Pico aspires to it:

> A certain sacred striving should seize the soul so that, not content with the indifferent and middling, we may pant after the highest and so (for we can if we want to) force our way up to it with all our might. Let us despise the terrestrial, be unafraid of the heavenly, and then, neglecting the things of the world, fly towards that court beyond the world nearest to God the Most High.
>
> (*On the Dignity of Man*)

With *Doctor Faustus* almost the reverse is true: transgression is born not of a liberating sense of freedom to deny or retrieve origin, nor from an excess of life breaking repressive bounds. It is rather a transgression rooted in an *impasse* of despair.

Even before he abjures God, Faustus expresses a sense of being isolated and trapped; an insecurity verging on despair preexists a damnation which, by a perverse act of free will, he "chooses." Arrogant he certainly is, but it is wrong to see Faustus at the outset as secure in the knowledge that existing forms of knowledge are inadequate. Rather, his search for a more complete knowledge is itself a search for security. For Faustus, "born, of parents base of stock," and now both socially and geographically displaced (Prologue, ll. 11, 13–19), no teleological integration of identity, self-consciousness and purpose obtains. In the opening scene he attempts to convince himself of the worth of several professions—divin-

ity, medicine, law, and then divinity again—only to reject each in turn;
in this he is almost schizoid:

> Having commenc'd, be a divine in show,
> Yet level at the end of every art,
> And live and die in Aristotle's works.
> Sweet Analytics, 'tis thou hast ravish'd me!
>
> When all is done, divinity is best.
>
> Philosophy is odious and obscure,
> Both law and physic are for petty wits,
> Divinity is basest of the three,
> Unpleasant, harsh, contemptible, and vile.
> (1.3–6, 37, 105–8)

As he shakes free of spurious orthodoxy and the role of the conventional
scholar, Faustus's insecurity intensifies. A determination to be "resolved"
of all ambiguities, to be "resolute" and show fortitude (1.32; 3.14; 5.6;
6.32, 64) is only a recurring struggle to escape agonised irresolution.

This initial desperation and insecurity, just as much as a subsequent
fear of impending damnation, suggests why his search for knowledge so
easily lapses into hedonistic recklessness and fatuous, self-forgetful "delight" (1.52; 5.82; 6.170; 8.59–60). Wagner cannot comprehend this psychology of despair:

> I think my master means to die shortly:
> He has made his will and given me his wealth
>
> I wonder what he means. If death were nigh,
> He would not banquet and carouse and swill
> Amongst the students.
> (18.1–2, 5–7)

Faustus knew from the outset what he would eventually incur. He willingly "surrenders up . . . his soul" for twenty-four years of "voluptuousness" in the knowledge that "eternal death" will be the result (3.90–94).
At the end of the first scene he exits declaring, "This night I'll conjure
though I die therefor." Later he reflects: "Long ere this I should have
done the deed [i.e., suicide] / Had not sweet pleasure conquer'd deep
despair" (6.24–25). This is a despairing hedonism rooted in the fatalism
of his opening soliloquy: "If we say that we have no sin, we deceive

ourselves, and there's no truth in us. Why, then, belike we must sin, and so consequently die" (1.41–44). Half-serious, half-facetious, Faustus registers a sense of humankind as miscreated.

Tamburlaine's will to power leads to liberation through transgression. Faustus's pact with the devil, because an act of transgression without hope of liberation, is at once rebellious, masochistic and despairing. The protestant God—"an arbitrary and wilful, omnipotent and universal tyrant" (Walzer, *The Revolution of the Saints*)—demanded of each subject that s/he submit personally and without mediation. The modes of power formerly incorporated in mediating institutions and practices now devolve on Him and, to some extent and unintentionally, on His subject: abject before God, the subject takes on a new importance in virtue of just this direct relation. Further, although God is remote and inscrutable he is also intimately conceived: "The principal worship of God hath two parts. One is to yield subjection to him, the other to draw near to him and to cleave unto him" (Perkins, *An Instruction Touching Religious or Divine Worship*). Such perhaps are the conditions for masochistic transgression: intimacy becomes the means of a defiance of power, the new-found importance of the subject the impetus of that defiance, the abjectness of the subject its self-sacrificial nature. (We may even see here the origins of subcultural transgression: the identity conferred upon the deviant by the dominant culture enables resistance as well as oppression.)

Foucault has written: "Limit and transgression depend on each other for whatever density of being they possess: a limit could not exist if it were absolutely uncrossable and, reciprocally, transgression would be pointless if it merely crossed a limit composed of illusions and shadows" (*Language, Counter-Memory, Practice*). It is a phenomenon of which the anti-essentialist writers of the Renaissance were aware: "Superiority and inferiority, maistry and subjection, are joyntly tied unto a naturall kinde of envy and contestation; they must perpetually enter-spoile one another" (Montaigne, *Essays*).

In the morality plays sin tended to involve blindness to the rightness of God's law, while repentance and redemption involved a renewed apprehension of it. In *Doctor Faustus* however sin is not the error of fallen judgement but a conscious and deliberate transgression of limit. It is a limit which, among other things, renders God remote and inscrutable yet subjects the individual to constant surveillance and correction; which holds the individual subject terrifyingly responsible for the fallen human condition while disallowing him or her any subjective power of redemption. Out of such conditions is born a mode of transgression identifiably protestant in origin: despairing yet defiant, masochistic yet wilful. Faustus is abject yet his is an abjectness which is strangely inseparable from arrogance, which reproaches the authority which demands it, which is not so much subdued as incited by that same authority:

> FAUSTUS: I gave . . . my soul for my cunning.
> ALL: God forbid!
> FAUSTUS: God forbade it indeed; but Faustus hath done it.
> (19.61–64)

Mephostophilis well understands transgressive desire; it is why he does not deceive Faustus about the reality of hell. It suggests too why he conceives of hell in the way he does; although his sense of it as a state of being and consciousness can be seen as a powerful recuperation of hell at a time when its material existence as a *place* of future punishment was being questioned, it is also an arrogant appropriation of hell, an incorporating of it into the consciousness of the subject.

A ritual pact advances a desire which cancels fear long enough to pass the point of no return:

> Lo, Mephostophilis, for love of thee
> Faustus hath cut his arm, and with his proper blood
> Assures his soul to be great Lucifer's,
> Chief lord and regent of perpetual night.
> View here this blood that trickles from mine arm,
> And let it be propitious for my wish.
> (5.54–58)

But his blood congeals, preventing him from signing the pact. Mephostophilis exits to fetch "fire to dissolve it." It is a simple yet brilliant moment of dramatic suspense, one which invites us to dwell on the full extent of the violation about to be enacted. Faustus finally signs but only after the most daring blasphemy of all: "Now will I make an end immediately / . . . *Consummatum est:* this bill is ended" (5.72–74). In transgressing utterly and desperately God's law, he appropriates Christianity's supreme image of masochistic sacrifice: Christ dying on the cross—and his dying words (cf. John 19:30). Faustus is not liberating himself, he is ending himself: "It is finished." Stephen Greenblatt is surely right to find in Marlowe's work "a subversive identification with the alien," one which "flaunts society's cherished orthodoxies, embraces what the culture finds loathsome or frightening." But what is also worth remarking about this particular moment is the way that a subversive identification with the alien is achieved and heightened through travesty of one such cherished orthodoxy.

POWER AND THE UNITARY SOUL

For Augustine the conflict which man experiences is not (as the Manichean heresy insisted) between two contrary souls or two contrary substances—rather, one soul fluctuates between contrary wills. On some occasions *Doctor Faustus* clearly assumes the Augustinian conception of the soul; on others—those expressive of or consonant with the Manichean implications of universal conflict—it presents Faustus as divided and, indeed, constituted by that division. The distinction which Augustine makes between the will as opposed to the soul as the site of conflict and division may now seem to be semantic merely; in fact it was and remains of the utmost importance. For one thing, as *Doctor Faustus* makes clear, the unitary soul—unitary in the sense of being essentially indivisible and eternal—is the absolute precondition for the exercise of divine power:

> O, no end is limited to damned souls.
> Why wert thou not a creature wanting soul?
> Or why is this immortal that thou hast?
> Ah, Pythagoras' *metempsychosis,* were that true,
> This soul should fly from me and I be chang'd
> Unto some brutish beast: all beasts are happy,
> For when they die
> Their souls are soon dissolv'd in elements;
> But mine must live still to be plagu'd in hell.
> (19.171–79)

Further, the unitary soul—unitary now in the sense of being essentially incorruptible—figures even in those manifestations of Christianity which depict the human condition in the most pessimistic of terms and human freedom as thereby intensely problematic. In a passage quoted below, the English Calvinist William Perkins indicates why, even for a theology as severe as his, this had to be so: if sin were a corruption of man's "substance" then not only could he not be immortal (and thereby subjected to the eternal torment which Faustus incurs), but Christ could not have taken on his nature.

Once sin or evil is allowed to penetrate to the core of God's subject (as opposed to being, say, an inextricable part of that subject's fallen *condition*) the most fundamental contradiction in Christian theology is reactivated: evil is of the essence of God's creation. This is of course only a more extreme instance of another familiar problem: How is evil possible in a world created by an omnipotent God? To put the blame on Adam only begs the further question: Why did God make Adam potentially evil? (Compare Nashe's impudent gloss: "Adam never fell till God made fools" [*The Unfortunate Traveller*].)

Calvin, however, comes close to allowing what Perkins and Augustine felt it necessary to deny: evil and conflict do penetrate to the core of God's subject. For Calvin the soul is an essence, immortal and created by God. But to suggest that it partakes of *God's* essence is a "monstrous" blasphemy: "If the soul of man is a portion transmitted from the essence of God, the divine nature must not only be liable to passion and change, but also to ignorance, evil desires, infirmity, and all kinds of vice" (*Institutes of the Christian Religion*). Given the implication that these imperfections actually constitute the soul, it is not surprising that "everyone feels that the soul itself is a receptacle for all kinds of pollution." Elsewhere we are told that the soul, "teeming with . . . seeds of vice . . . is altogether devoid of good." Here is yet another stress point in protestantism and one which plays like *Doctor Faustus* (and *Mustapha*) exploit: if human beings perpetuate disorder it is because they have been created disordered.

The final chorus of the play tells us that Dr Faustus involved himself with "unlawful things" and thereby practised "more than heavenly power permits" (ll. 6, 8). It is a transgression which has revealed the limiting structure of Faustus's universe for what it is, namely, "heavenly *power*." Faustus has to be destroyed since in a very real sense the credibility of that heavenly power depends upon it. And yet the punitive intervention which validates divine power also compromises it: far from justice, law and authority being what legitimates power, it appears, by the end of the play, to be the other way around: power establishes the limits of all those things.

It might be objected that the distinction between justice and power is a modern one and, in Elizabethan England, even if entertained, would be easily absorbed in one or another of the paradoxes which constituted the Christian faith. And yet: if there is one thing that can be said with certainty about this period it is that God in the form of "mere arbitrary will omnipotent" could not "keep men in awe." We can infer as much from many texts, one of which was Lawne's *Abridgement* of Calvin's *Institutes,* translated in 1587—around the time of the writing of *Doctor Faustus.* The book presents and tries to answer, in dialogue form, objections to Calvin's theology. On the question of predestination the "Objector" contends that "to adjudge to destruction whom he will, is more agreeable to the lust of a tyrant, than to the lawful sentence of a judge." The "Reply" to this is as arbitrary and tyrannical as the God which the Objector envisages as unsatisfactory: "It is a point of bold wickedness even so much as to inquire the causes of God's will." It is an exchange which addresses directly the question of whether a tyrannical God is or is not grounds for discontent. Even more important perhaps is its unintentional foregrounding of the fact that, as embodiment of naked power alone, God could so easily be collapsed into those tyrants who, we are repeatedly told by writers in this period, exploited Him as ideological mystification of their own power. Not surprisingly, the concept of "heavenly power" interrogated in Doctor Faustus was soon to lose credibility, and it did so in part precisely because of such interrogation.

Doctor Faustus is important for subsequent tragedy for these reasons and at least one other: in transgressing and demystifying the limiting structure of his world without there ever existing the possibility of his escaping it, Faustus can be seen as an important precursor of the malcontented protagonist of Jacobean tragedy. Only for the latter, the limiting structure comes to be primarily a sociopolitical one.

Lastly, if it is correct that censorship resulted in Doctor Faustus being one of the last plays of its kind—it being forbidden thereafter to interrogate religious issues so directly—we might expect the transgressive impulse in the later plays to take on different forms. This is in fact exactly what we do find; and one such form involves a strategy already referred to—the inscribing of a subversive discourse within an orthodox one, a vindication of the letter of an orthodoxy while subverting its spirit.

Doctor Faustus and Hell on Earth

Christopher Ricks

F. W. Bateson, the scholar-critic, was a contextualist. One particular context for Marlowe's *Doctor Faustus* is so obvious as to have become largely
invisible. A sense of it may do something to meet the complaint of Wilbur
Sanders that the play is "chronically over-explicit," and even to meet
Sanders's further predicament: "It is a nagging sense that there is some
more broadly-based and more humanly intelligible way of looking at the
Faustian predicament . . . that makes me reluctant to call *Doctor Faustus*
a great play."

William Empson often sought the more broadly based and more
humanly intelligible way of looking at works of literature by suggesting
that, far from our being faced by the "over-explicit," there was something about the plot which had become obscured. "I think the point was
obvious at the time, so obvious that it did not get stated in the text,"
Empson says of his suggestion that in *The Spanish Tragedy* "Andrea had
been murdered for love." Similarly, of Joyce's *Ulysses* Empson posits the
offering of Molly by Bloom to Stephen, and then is sweetly reasonable
about the substantiation: "Last of the list, the textual evidence for the
Bloom Offer should now be given. There is none to give, as Bloom feels
that plain words would put Stephen off, or give him an excuse for a
refusal; but I could not think that this upsets the theory." *Ulysses* is then
one kind of extreme case of something's being importantly unstated,
since the Bloom Offer is both obvious and a secret: "Why then does the
book make a secret of it? Because the procedure which it regards as an
innocent act of charity is heavily penalised by the law. A sexual act per-

From *Essays in Criticism* 35, no. 2 (April 1985). © 1985 by Christopher Ricks.

formed by two people in the presence of a third one, whatever their sexes, counts as 'gross indecency.' Prosecutions are seldom mounted, as any eye-witness confesses to the offence automatically." "Mounted" has its glint.

The plot of *Doctor Faustus*, too, made Empson think. Mephistophilis says of the trapped Faustus:

> his labouring brain
> Begets a world of idle fantasies
> To overreach the devil; but all in vain.
> (19.13–15)

The rhyme is grimly conclusive. Empson, asking himself how it could be that an unstupid Faustus could have made so stupid a bargain, set his own labouring brain to beget a world of not-idle fantasies as to how and why Faustus might ever have supposed that he could overreach the devil. Empson even engaged in one supreme kind of practical criticism, the writing of a passage of verse which, interpolated in the text, would make cogent his, Empson's, interpretation of the play. In a letter to me in 1976 (which I quote with the kind permission of Lady Empson), Empson said:

> all?
> I have written a bit more for the chorus introducing Act II, usually starting with the soliloquy *Now Faustus must thou needs be damned:*

> > Faustus would overreach the Devil now
> > And work the spirits yet not pay in Hell.
> > He fancies they are doubledealing him
> > Claiming Hell's grandeur for a fantasy—
> > Not making much of Mephistophilis
> > Thinks him a spirit of the elements,
> > Until he sees the face of Lucifer.
> > He offers murder, but in words alone,
> > As meet to flatter Mephistophilis;
> > Not after he has seen great Lucifer.

> Then the meeting with the other magicians, and the start of the soliloquy after they have gone, are in prose, resuming at "Despair in God." I hope my Faust gets performed, but writing the jolly scene in the Sultan's harem will be delayed as long as possible.

"*Usually* starting with the soliloquy" is deliciously cool. But this too is a different type of the extreme case, Empson being obliged to write a passage (of extraordinary ageless nonpastiche, it must be said) without which his thesis about the play will not be credited. The new lines don't just give the argument a leg up, they give it a leg to stand on.

Such suppositions about a plot within a work are usually more vulnerable than suppositions about what presses upon a work from without. Recent critical theory, with its "margins," might have its own ways of exfoliating Empson's point about *The Ancient Mariner,* for instance; a point not about the poem's plot but about its contemporary context. Empson argued, among other things, that the slave-trade impinges upon the poem. What great guilt so preoccupied Coleridge during those years? What is the great guilt that attaches to the heroic maritime expansions? For the slave-trade may be one of the three or four monstrosities so great as to make any direct contemplation and realization in art unthinkable (hideously rivalled by the death-camps and by atomic devastation). The best poem that deals with the slave-trade (perhaps the only good poem?) would then not be about it; rather, the slave-trade would be about the poem. For Empson would not have wished to speak of the slave-trade as the subject of *The Ancient Mariner,* but nor would he have wished to square it as a mere frame. It is rather one of the poem's elements. It is in the air.

What was in the air for the early audiences of *Doctor Faustus* was the plague.

Bateson saw that "with *Piers Plowman, Troilus and Criseyde,* the *Canterbury Tales,* and *Sir Gawain and the Green Knight,* English literature suddenly came of age": "It cannot be a coincidence that this literature all belongs to the generation immediately succeeding the bubonic pandemic of 1348–49 that is now known as the Black Death. . . . A society that loses one third of its population in some fifteen months must adjust itself violently if it is to survive" (*A Guide to English Literature*). The plague was to be endemic in England after the Black Death. Everyone knows about the plague in Marlowe's London, but apparently no one chooses to bring it into substantial relation to *Doctor Faustus;* not even F. P. Wilson, author of *The Plague in Shakespeare's London* and of *Marlowe and the Early Shakespeare,* and editor of Dekker's Plague Pamphlets. The pressure of the plague upon the play strikes me as obvious and yet ignored. A *cordon sanitaire* has been left between *Doctor Faustus* and even the biographical facts or likelihoods. Plague was so rife then that the less likely choice, for the play's composition, of 1588–89 rather than 1592–93 would not much matter. Still, 1592–93—the last year of Marlowe's life—has more to be said for it. W. W. Greg noted that the play "was performed, presumably on the London stage, by some unidentified company, no doubt before the plague of 1592–94 reached its height and put a stop to all acting. In May 1593, Marlowe was at Thomas Walsingham's country house, "having perhaps taken refuge there from the plague which was raging in London" (John Jump).

Marlowe's personal involvement with the plague would matter less than everyone's involvement with it. Even to speak of a "context" is to understate what is at issue. Keith Thomas's title for the Prologue to *Religion and the Decline of Magic* is "The Environment," and he at once gives the plague a hideous pride of place:

> Most dreaded of all was the bubonic plague, which was en-
> demic until the last quarter of the seventeenth century. . . . In
> the hundred and fifty years before the great visitation of 1665
> there were only a dozen years when London was free from
> plague. Some people were thought to have died of it every year
> and periodically there were massive outbreaks. . . . In 1563
> some 20,000 Londoners are thought to have died; in 1593,
> 15,000. . . . The plague terrified by its suddenness, its viru-
> lence and its social effects.

Even the words "The Environment," though far less abstract and academic than my speaking of a "context," have here too much equanimity. The plague horrifyingly environs you, but then—even worse—you environ it.

The plague then pressed everywhere in the city, as the plague-orders will evidence (perhaps first printed 1574; an important collection in 1583; 1592 . . .). But the plague pressed notoriously upon the theatre. F. P. Wilson devotes a separate section to this: "The Elizabethan theatres suffered heavily from the many epidemics of the sixteenth and seventeenth centuries." The City wrote to the Privy Council (ca. 1584): "To play in plague-time is to increase the plague by infection: to play out of plague-time is to draw the plague by offendings of God upon occasion of such plays." *Play* tolls with *plague* (guilt by association and infection), in a way which must have left French preachers envious (*la peste* having no such tolling against French plays); and so it does again in a sermon of 1577: "The cause of plagues is sinne, if you looke to it well: and the cause of sinne are plays: therefore the cause of plagues are playes." "The reward of sin is death."

Even those who did not think that the plague was God's wrath against plays must still have conceded that, for other reasons, the authorities were right to close the theatres, as they so often did from 1564 on. Wilson quotes the Court of Aldermen in 1583 on the danger of "the assembly of people to plays . . . and many infected with sores running on them . . . perilous for contagion . . . the terrible occasion of God's wrath and heavy striking with plagues." The assembly of people to church-services was a shifty matter: "The authorities," Wilson notes drily, "for the most part held that it was impossible to take the infection during the act of worship, but their regulations do not tally with their convictions." Some of the fierceness with which churchmen attacked the theatres is likely to be an unease at such odious comparisons. By the time there appeared, in 1604, "the earliest edition of the play of which a copy has survived," a huge and hideous failure to survive had supervened: the plague of 1603, *The Wonderfull yeare* in the title of Dekker's lacerating account, when 36,000 died, over a sixth of the inhabitants of London. Three years later, and not without memories of *Doctor Faustus,* Dekker gave to the world *The Seven Deadly Sinnes of London, Drawn in seven severall coaches, through the seven severall Gates of the Citie, Bringing the Plague with them* (1606). Edward Arber's nineteenth-century reprint, prefacing the work with "The Scheme of the Triumphs of the Seven Deadly Sins of London," produced a sentence which has its aptness to *Doctor Faustus* as I see it: "The Plague is threatened, but not described; having been so recently experienced."

It is doubtful whether an audience at any play performed in 1594 and soon thereafter could extirpate the consciousness that plague was in the air. Plague was even to put in bizarre appearances in *Volpone* and *The Alchemist.* But in any case Marlowe, with decisiveness and tact, immediately intimates the plague's importance without letting it become the subject of the play (it is the play's element, not its subject). For what is Faustus's triumph as a doctor, there in the twenty-first line of the play's first scene?

> Are not thy bills hung up as monuments,
> Whereby whole cities have escap'd the plague?

—with *plague* given the salience of rhythmical conclusion, and yet (here is the tact) not left there—not pressed, but touched:

> Whereby whole cities have escap'd the plague
> And thousand desperate maladies been cur'd?

Cur'd is exactly stationed against *the plague;* you escape the plague, or you don't—cures are something else. An audience in these years, in a theatre of all places, would not have taken lightly a reference, twenty lines into a play, to medicine's mastery as that "Whereby whole cities have escap'd the plague." Nor would they have taken lightly (as we do, when we say that we avoid something like the plague, or talk of being pestered), that oath which recurs in *Doctor Faustus:* "A plague on her"; "A plague take you" (four times, this last or a form of it). The centre of the play is visited by these curses; the beginning and end of the play speak of the visitation of the plague itself, which thereby swathes the play. First, the literal plague of the first scene; last, the eternal plague that is Hell. Faustus had cursed his enemies ("And hell shall after plague their treachery"), and at the very end, twelve lines before his last words, he contemplates his undying soul: "But mine must live still to be plagu'd in hell." Let us at least think of what it was to live in terror of the plague, and in terror of Hell; and let us (later) think too of their likeness and unlikeness.

But first it must be stressed not only that the world of Marlowe and of the theatre was alive to plague but that so is *The History of Doctor Faustus* (translated 1592, and either Marlowe's source or—less likely—derived from a source shared with Marlowe). Three of the *History's* chapters refer literally to plague, and two others have the extended sense ("as plagues unto men," "plaguing us"). Faustus had powers of prediction for which in Marlowe's England men would have given much: "If anything wonderful were at hand, as death, famine, plague, or wars, he would set the time and place in true and just order, when it should come to pass" (chap. 17). Not, again, that there is anything surprising about this connection, which would rather have about it a tacit obviousness amounting to inevitability. For the Devil was intimate with plague. In *The Hour of Our Death,* Philippe Ariès has a section on (a happy conjunction) "The Influence of the Missionaries and of the Plague"; and in "The Visit to the Cemetery" he expatiates on the plague as "the work of the devil"; "For the devil extends his power in time of plague. . . . The plague, the devil, and the cemetery form a kind of unholy trinity of influence." In the plague-ridden London of Marlowe's day, people knew just how diabolical was the notorious longing for company felt by the damned. When Faustus elicits from Mephistophilis the reason why the devils crave to enlarge their kingdom—*Solamen miseris socios habuisse doloris* (To the unhappy, it is a comfort to have had companions in misfortune)—the thought would have struck with particular force upon those who knew one diabolical horror of the plague: that, as Defoe was later to say in *A Journal of the Plague Year,* "there was a seeming propensity or a wicked inclination in those that were infected to infect others."

To feel the pressure of the plague upon the play is to gain a different sense of much about Faustus's bargain and about the exercises of power which follow it—or rather, about how both of these matters would have been likely to strike the contemporary audience. There is a long tradition of mere disparagement of Faustus's bargain, a tradition which gravitates naturally from a sense that Faustus demeans himself to a sense that *Doctor Faustus* demeans itself. Francis Jeffrey spoke of Faustus's selling his soul "for the ordinary price of sensual pleasure" [in *Marlowe,* Doctor Faustus: *A Casebook,* ed. John Jump]; L. C. Knights, of "the perverse and infantile desire for enormous power and immediate gratifications." In his Revels edition, John Jump exhibits this conventional wisdom, which of course has a lot of truth in it: "Faustus, then, concludes an infamous bargain in order to enjoy the knowledge, the pleasure, and above all the power for which he craves." But to say only this is to ignore the greatest and most fundamental thing which Faustus buys with his soul, so great and fundamental as to go unnoticed if we are not careful: the guarantee that he will live for another twenty-four years. Such a guarantee would never be nugatory (and critics are oddly blithe who write as if it would be), but it must come with particular force in times of, say, war and—even more— in time of plague. In the midst of life we are in death: this was monstrously manifest in a society haunted by plague. Faustus, in buying those years (a span of years which would at his age take him up to about the life-expectancy of Elizabethan England—a great many young adults died in their prime between twenty and fifty), could not but be a manifestation of a guarantee which even the most devout must sometimes crave and which all, in those years, might especially crave.

When Wilbur Sanders says that "Faustus's condemnation is . . . writ large (too large, as I see it) in the opening scene," I should want to stay a little with the word "condemnation," and relate it to the pressure then of being condemned to sudden death. Faustus is plainly condemned by the play; but we make this too easy for ourselves, too untaxing, if we abstract Faustus's decision from a world which would at least have been more than usually *tempted* (the notion is dramatically and spiritually apt) to condone all such bargains as, in extremis, tried to buy sheer life. G. H. Lewes's words are touched with complacency: "a legend admirably characteristic of the spirit of those ages in which men, believing in the agency of the devil, would willingly have bartered their future existence for the satisfaction of present desires." But Faustus, when he mortgages his post-mortal life (*not* barters his future *existence,* exactly), buys with it not just the satisfaction of present desires, but a guarantee of twenty-four years of precisely "future existence." Hazlitt may say that, in order to "realise all the fictions of a lawless imagination," Faustus "sets at defiance all mortal consequences," but *mortal* consequences are just what Faustus precludes for twenty-four years. It is all very well for Hazlitt to deplore the bargain, but his words "for a few short years" are unimaginative. How short is short, and how few is few? Hazlitt is not really contemplating sequent death. The point is not that Faustus is shown as under such sentence of sudden death, but that his tragedy was devised for an audience who would inform it with their own sense of such a visitation, and who would therefore not sell short, as being sold "for a few short years," the fearful impulses with which the play is in touch. Most of us, even young scholars, would not simply or entirely despise a guarantee of twenty-four years of life; the more so, in a society where life-expectancy was markedly less than in ours; and *a fortiori* in a society ravaged by plague. The most thoroughgoing excoriation of Faustus is by James Smith; the essay has all of Smith's fierce clarity and theological edge, and it twice speaks of Faustus as not having "the shadow of an excuse." But it is a consequence of Smith's merciless position that he should not ever ask about one shadow which might fall upon the play as first performed ("Whereby whole cities have escap'd the plague"), a shadow which would constitute at least the relevant *temptation* to see an excuse; just as it is a consequence of Smith's position that he should make no mention whatsoever of Faustus's aspirations and achievements in medicine.

For the most important function of the middle scenes of the play is their explicit insistence upon Faustus's being, for his twenty-four years, incapable of dying. My word "function" carries the traditional reservation about these scenes, which are often unimaginative in conception and feeble in execution. But execution is the word. When the play (in its B text) took over from *The History of Doctor Faustus* the revenge-stories—of the Knight Benvolio with his horns, and of the horse-courser—it took over stories which turn upon the impossibility of killing Faustus. But the play is explicit where the *History* is not, for it is only in the play that Faustus is given this to say, when his head had seemed to be struck from his shoulders:

> Knew you not, traitors, I was limited
> For four-and-twenty years to breathe on earth?

And had you cut my body with your swords,
Or hew'd this flesh and bones as small as sand,
Yet in a minute had my spirit return'd
And I had breath'd a man made free from harm.
But wherefore do I dally my revenge?

(13.71–76)

It is a mere six lines later that Faustus exults, imprudently and blasphemously, in divine vengeance ("And hell shall after plague their treachery"); and it is this speech—"I was limited / For four-and-twenty years to breathe on earth"—which makes clear how the play takes the pre-eminent contractual item, on Faustus's side of the bargain, which is adapted from the *History:* "On these conditions following: First, that Faustus may be a spirit in form and substance." That is, incapable of mortality. "Yet in a minute had my spirit return'd / And I had breath'd a man made free from harm."

The divine peripety is such that everything which makes for Faustus makes also against him. The unkillability which is a mercy when he loathes others is a torment when he loathes himself; it is one of the tacitly horrible things about Faustus's impulse to commit suicide that suicide is not his to commit:

"Faustus, thou art damn'd! Then guns and knives,
Swords, poison, halters, and envenom'd steel
Are laid before me to dispatch myself;
And long ere this I should have done the deed
Had not sweet pleasure conquer'd deep despair.

(6.21–25)

He speaks too soon. No more than Spenser's Despair could Faustus kill himself.

Damn'd art thou, Faustus, damn'd; despair and die!

(Mephistophilis gives him a dagger)

Hell claims his right and with a roaring voice
Says, "Faustus, come; thine hour is almost come";
And Faustus now will come to do thee right.

(18.55–59)

But until his hour is come, Mephistophilis's dagger is cruelly—tantalisingly—absurd; and once his hour is come, no dagger will release him.

Faustus, then, buys not only knowledge and power, but time—half a lifetime of it, and this is to be put before an audience who knew with particular force that a lifetime might now be no time at all. In the words of the *History*, he buys "certain years to live"; and years certainly to live. Dekker wrote of the plague: "And albeit, no man at any time is assured of life, yet no man (within the memory of man) was ever so neere death as now." But Faustus was "assured of life." It is just that the premium was damnably steep. My claim is not that our apprehending this will make the play perfect but that it will make much of the play more explicable; the enterprise makes sense. Here I have in mind what I take to be the exemplary demonstration in our day of such a critical argument: the account of *Cymbeline*, and of the pressure put upon the play by King James's statecraft, by Emrys Jones; an account of "Stuart *Cymbeline*" which scrupulously distinguishes explanation from justification.

T. S. Eliot described Marlowe as "the most thoughtful, the most blasphemous (and therefore, probably, the most Christian)" of Shakespeare's contemporaries. One dimension of the blasphemy within the play is the hideous perversion, within the Faustian bargain, of the usual high and holy hope. The hope was that God and goodness would protect you; protect you even against the plague. On the other hand, mere underlings of the supernatural were likely to prove inadequate: "There was seldom any suggestion that a cunning man could cure a victim of the plague, though he might be able to give him a charm or amulet which would prevent him from catching it": Keith Thomas's words might be related to his insistence on the frequency of Faustian stories during the sixteenth and seventeenth centuries:

> Spirit-raising was a standard magical activity. Spiritual beings were thought to offer a short cut to riches, love, knowledge and power of all kinds; and the Faustian legend had a literal meaning for its Elizabethan and Jacobean audiences.
> (*Religion and the Decline of Magic*)

But if we give a literal meaning to "power of all kinds," it becomes clear that one such kind is the ground of all others. The supreme Faustian bargain could on occasion give a short cut to not being cut short.

"In times of plague, remarked an Elizabethan theologian, men 'flee for remedy. . . some to certain saints as S. Roch or S. Anthony; and some to the superstitious arts of witchcraft'" (Keith Thomas).

> Say he surrenders up to him his soul
> So he will spare him four-and-twenty years,
> Letting him live in all voluptuousness.
> (3.92–94)

Spare him, not only as granting him years, but as granting him clemency in the face of death. The same sense of first-things-first is tacit in the sequence of the line "Letting him live in all voluptuousness."

Doctor Faustus is a play not only about buying time and a guarantee of living to spend it, but about buying them with an eternity of Hell. Hell eternally vibrates with—to and against—the plague. For the plague was Hell on earth; it was both more hideously Hell than this earth had seen, and yet—just because it was on this earth—it fell hideously short of that eternity, not the less appalling for being inconceivable, of suffering. It is not anything so cool as a trope which leads the play to reiterate the conjunction:

> And hell shall after plague their treachery.
> (13.83)

> But mine must live still to be plagued in hell.
> (19.179)

Still: always. Take the worst suffering the earth has seen; take away from it the one thing which mitigates its terror, that it does end ("All's well that ends," in the happy amputation of Robert Lowell); and you are left with the plague's bitter likeness and ultimate unlikeness to Hell, such as struck more than the usual fear of God into people. "Ay, we must die an everlasting death" (1.45): a fate worse than death. When Dekker cried out, of the plague, "What miserie continues ever?" he sought comfort even within the plague. But the plague that is Hell (a plague made manifest in the sores and blains in the art of Bosch and Breughel) is all darkness visible and comfortless. It is the agonizing pincer-jaws of the divine paradox. Faustus "now must die eternally" (19.29). "Impose some end to my incessant pain" (19.168), he pleads, desperately contradicting himself in the very utterance.

No one can write about the plague as well as Dekker without calling up Hell on earth:

> What an unmatchable torment were it for a man to be bard
> up every night in a vast silent Charnell-house? hung (to make
> it more hideous) with lamps dimly & slowly burning, in hol-
> low and glimmering corners: where all the pavement should
> in stead of greene rushes, be strewde with blasted Rosemary,
> withered Hyacinthes, fatall Cipresse and Ewe, thickly mingled
> with heapes of dead mens bones: the bare ribbes of a father
> that begat him, lying there: here the Chaples hollow scull of

a mother that bore him: round about him a thousand Coarses, some standing bolt upright in their knotted winding sheetes: others halfe mouldred in rotten Coffins, that should suddenly yawne wide open, filling his nosthrils with noysome stench, and his eyes with the sight of nothing but crawling wormes . . . were not this an infernall prison? would not the strongest-harted man (beset with such a ghastly horror) looke wilde? and runne madde? and die? And even such a formidable shape did the diseased Citie appeare in.

Here, in *The Wonderfull yeare,* Dekker moves naturally, horribly so, from such an evocation of Hell on earth—"an infernall prison"—to a sermon on sin and mortality; to blasphemy; to tragedy ("the shutting up of this Tragicall Act"); and to the old undying mingling of fascination and exhaustion: "My spirit grows faint with rowing in this Stygian Ferry," but then at once:

Imagine then that all this while, Death (like a Spanish Leagar, or rather like stalking *Tamberlaine*) hath pitcht his tents, (being nothing but a heape of winding sheetes tackt together) in the sinfully-polluted Suburbes: the Plague is Muster-maister and Marshall of the field: Burning Feavers, Boyles, Blaines, and Carbuncles.

Why, this is Hell, nor am I out of it. And yet not so, for this—being within time, which is the mercy of eternity—is a Hell which men and women can die out of.

This knot—of the play and the plague, temporal and eternal—is drawn so tight by Marlowe that the binding strands are less visible than they are in lesser art, for instance that of George Wither's *History of the Pestilence* (1625):

And harke yee People, harken you, I pray,
That were wth me preserv'd to see this day:
And listen you, that shall be brought upon
This *Stage* of action, when our *Sceane* is done.
Come harken all, and lett no soule refraine
To heare; nor lett it heare my words in vayne.
ffor, from the slaughter house of *Death,* & from
The habitations of the *Dead,* I come.

> I am escaped from the greedie Iawes
> Of *Hell*.
>
> (1.31–40)

If the plague cannot be conceived of except as a type of Hell (and yet far short), then likewise Hell is brought home as plague. But in *Doctor Faustus* the words "perpetual" and "that ne'er can die" are admonitions that hereafter the last twist of the knife is that there will be no last twist of the knife:

> Now, Faustus, let thine eyes with horror stare
> Into that vast perpetual torture-house.
> There are the furies, tossing damned souls
> On burning forks; their bodies boil in lead:
> There are live quarters broiling on the coals,
> That ne'er can die.
>
> (19.116–21)

Wilbur Sanders deplores this "obsessive preoccupation with infernal torments": "It is one of those matters on which his imagination appears to have dwelt with unwholesome insistence." But the case is altered if the torments are not only infernal and not only imagined.

"No mortal can express the pains of Hell" (18.47)—not least because it is immortals who feel them. But the plague can express something, along with the sense of just what the inexpressibility amounts to.

> Inspire us therefore how to tell
> The *Horror* of a *Plague*, the *Hell*.
> (*Newes from Graves-ende*, 1604)

Inspire has its horrid power here. "Sicknes was sent to breathe her unwholesome ayres into thy nosthrils." For if plague was in the air, it was dangerous to breathe a word. Hence the grim comedy of certain of the "tokens," as Defoe was to acknowledge. "My friend Dr Heath was of opinion that it might be known by the smell of their breath; but then, as he said, who durst smell to that breath for his information? since, to know it, he must draw the stench of the plague up into his own brain, in order to distinguish the smell!"

John Berryman wrote in one of the Dream Songs (No. 366):

> These Songs are not meant to be understood, you understand.
> They are only meant to terrify & comfort.

Berryman was looking back at one of Dekker's Plague Pamphlets: *London*

Looke Backe, At That Yeare of Yeares 1625. And Looke Forward, Upon This Yeare, 1630: Written, not to Terrifie, But to Comfort. Marlowe's *Doctor Faustus* is aligned rather with Berryman's "&" than with Dekker's "not . . . But." It is written to terrify and comfort. The sources of the terror are not quite what is sometimes said; it is not "the possibility of final destruction" (Sanders) which is supremely appalling, but the final possibility that there is no such thing, instead an eternity of damnation, never final. "Thy fatal time draws to a final end" (15.22). Not final, but only temporarily finite, and to be succeeded by an infinite eternity of being plagued in Hell. The comfort, consolation even, is that which is characteristic of art, which must not be—in Frank Kermode's great phrase— "too consolatory to console." In time of plague, there can be imagined— even then—something worse: an eternity of plague. In time of plague, there can be imagined, too, something better: an eternity without plague. An eternity of Heaven, perhaps; or at least, not least, of oblivion. If the Christian vision is not true (Marlowe's great compliment to Christianity is not to believe it but to entertain it), our souls may be "chang'd into little water drops, / And fall into the ocean, ne'er be found" (19.185–86). Eliot, who paid Marlowe the compliment of believing him blasphemous, once argued with A. A. Milne about pacifism:

> I think . . . that writers like Mr. Milne suffer from two prejudices. One is that the great thing is to go on living. "If," he says "the intelligent man of war wishes to know why death is taken so seriously by so many people, I will tell him." After this portentous preparation, Mr. Milne stops for an impressive moment (indicated by a new paragraph) and continues: "The reason is this: Death is final. . . . Death is the worst thing that can happen, because it is the last thing that can happen." Well, I felicitate Mr. Milne; he is haunted neither by the thought of Achilles among the shades, nor by the terrors of death that beset the Christian. "Death is final." If I thought that death was final, it would seem to me a far less serious matter than it does. I should still no doubt be afraid of dying (though tired of living, as Mr. Paul Robeson sang), but I should not be afraid of death. And life would seem to me much less important than it does.
>
> (*Time and Tide,* January 12, 1935)

Marlowe's *Doctor Faustus* takes the plague more seriously than might

seem from the plot alone. So does Goethe's *Faust*. Goethe's social satire
against fashionable medicine may seem airy light:

> But above all, learn to handle women!
> Their everlasting moans and groans,
> So multifarious, miscellaneous,
> Are cured at a single point.
>> (trans. Randall Jarrell)

But everlasting moans and groans call up another scene. This grim levity
of an impersonating Mephistophilis is reached only after we have passed
through the extraordinary story of the plague. First, there is the Old
Peasant's gratitude to Faust and his father:

> Many a man stands living here
> That your father, in the nick of time,
> Snatched from the fever's burning rage
> When he put limits to the plague.
> And you yourself, a young man then,
> Went into every stricken house:
> Many a corpse they took away
> But you, though, came out safe and sound
> And bore up under bitter trials.
> The Helper yonder gave our helper aid.

More bitter, though, is the diabolical truth:

> I thought to extort from the Lord in Heaven
> This ending of that plague. The crowd's applause
> Sounds to me, now, like mockery.
> Oh, if only you could look into my soul:
> How little father and son deserve such fame!

> There was the medicine! The patients died
> And no one asked: But who's recovered?

> And so with hellish electuaries
> Worse, far worse, than the plague itself,
> We raged through these mountains and these valleys.
> I myself have given poison to thousands.
> They withered away—and I must live
> To hear men praise the shameless murderers!

Goethe's Faust is one by whom whole cities have incurred the plague, and thousand desperate maladies been caused.

Again, when Thomas Mann turned to a modern *Doctor Faustus,* it was natural to him to recur repeatedly to the plague. The Devil's insinuating conversation with Adrian Leverkühn turns naturally to a memory of the plague at Cologne, just as witchcraft is here more than once called a pestilence. A modern *Doctor Faustus* inevitably makes explicit the sex-horror (of which D. H. Lawrence wrote so penetratingly) attendant upon that subspecies of the plague which was thought to invite the larger plague: venereal disease. When Mann's Devil invokes "running sore and plague and worm-eaten nose" (chap. 25), he conjures up a venereal plague. When Leverkühn in his illness is "pinched and plagued with hot pincers" (chap. 33), these anticipate the plagues of Hell. Such a conjunction had been manifest in Marlowe's understanding of Faust and lust, and in others of the age. John Donne has a hot punitive lust upon him when in a sermon on the plague he relishes the fact of "men whose lust carried them into the jaws of infection in lewd houses, and seeking one sore perished with another." Dekker more than once sees the plague as a diseased whore. If we seek a modern counterpart to the plague, we have it, horribly to hand, in the ungrounded panic and the grounded terror of AIDS.

Mann's novel is, too, a reminder of the way in which art—in the face of the greatest horrors (plague, the slave-trade, the death-camps)— may be obliged by indirections to find directions out. For even as the plague is not Marlowe's subject but his environment and element, so the Nazi horror, with its culmination in the death-camps, is Mann's pressure and oppression. "Yet how strangely the times, these very times in which I write, are linked with the period that forms the frame of this biography!" Those words come two pages after the novel itself has cracked open:

> A transatlantic general has forced the population of Weimar to file past the crematories of the neighbouring concentration-camp. He declared that these citizens—who had gone in apparent righteousness about their daily concerns and sought to know nothing, although the wind brought to their noses the stench of burning human flesh—he declared that they too were guilty of the abominations on which he forced them now to turn their eyes. Was that unjust? Let them look, I look with them. In spirit I let myself be shouldered in their dazed or

shuddering ranks. Germany had become a thick-walled underground torture-chamber, converted into one by a profligate dictatorship vowed to nihilism from its beginnings on. Now the torture-chamber has been broken open, open lies our shame before the eyes of the world. Foreign commissions inspect those incredible photographs everywhere displayed, and tell their countrymen that what they have seen surpasses in horribleness anything the human imagination can conceive.

(trans. H. T. Lowe-Porter)

Why, this is Hell. It remains the central critical question about Mann's *Doctor Faustus* whether it did achieve a true relation of those horrors to the Faustian legend. "Needing Hell, we have learned how to build and run it on earth," says George Steiner, musing upon the price we may have paid for "the loss of Hell." "The absence of the familiar damned opened a vortex which the modern totalitarian state filled." Some of us, though, think that the presence of the familiar damned did not do much exactly to stanch the Inquisition and its lively work at enacting Hell on earth. Rather a Christian country, Germany.

Let me end, then, with a work which contemplates Hell (and totalitarianism), but with a reversal of the figure and ground as I see them in Marlowe: *The Plague* of Albert Camus. Its essential context, or again element, is not here the subject of the novel: totalitarian evil in general, and Nazi anti-semitism in particular. When Camus first set down notes for the novel, the nightmare consummation of this evil had not yet brought about the death-camps. Yet Camus as early as 1941 saw the association of the plague with anti-semitism; he noted that "in 1342 . . . at the time of the Black Death, Jews were executed. In 1481, when the plague ravaged southern Spain, the Inquisition blamed the Jews." When Camus's novel was published in 1947, it could be seen as more truly responsive to the vile genocide than any direct engagement in art had been. The man who jotted down in 1941 the disconcerting words *La Peste libératrice* did not stay in thrall to the perverted religious asseverations of Antonin Artaud, who craved the plague as a great cleanser and was sure that "the theatre is like the plague." Yet Artaud's argument, in "Theatre and the Plague," does rise, in its dementia, to being blasphemy; as Camus's novel, in its sanity, rises to being a work of art which engages with a supreme horror, of Hell on earth and elsewhere, by not allowing the horror to practise the subjections of being the subject—any more than Marlowe had yielded to the pressure of the plague. "I, too, believe in

calling things by their name. . . . But what's the name in this case?"
"That I shan't say; and anyhow you wouldn't gain anything by knowing." But we who hear this conversation in *The Plague* know what is not
being said. "The doctor was still looking out of the window. Beyond it
lay the tranquil radiance of a cool spring sky; inside the room a word
was echoing still, the word 'plague.'" In Marlowe's *Doctor Faustus*, it
echoes, but from outside too, though from no tranquil radiance: "O, it
strikes, it strikes!"

Chronology

1564	Christopher Marlowe born in Canterbury to John Marlowe, a cobbler. Christened at the church of St. George the Martyr, Canterbury, on February 26.
1579–80	Scholar at the King's School, Canterbury.
1580–87	Attends Corpus Christi College, Cambridge. Awarded a Parker scholarship for his years at Cambridge; presumably he was expected to be preparing for holy orders. Receives his B.A. in 1584. Graduates with an M.A. after intervention of Queen's Privy Council. Goes to London.
1587	*Tamburlaine,* parts 1 and 2, performed by Lord Admiral's Men, with Edward Alleyn in title role.
1589	Arrested in a street brawl, briefly imprisoned in Newgate.
1590	Publication of parts 1 and 2 of *Tamburlaine.*
1592	Bound over to keep the peace. Although he must have been writing *Faustus, The Jew of Malta, Edward II,* and *The Massacre at Paris* during these last few years (*Dido* may well have been written while he was at Cambridge), there are no reliable dates either for the composition or the chronological sequence of these plays.
1593	The Privy Council issues a warrant for his arrest on May 18, six days after his friend Thomas Kyd has been arrested on suspicion of treason and has, under torture, accused Marlowe of atheism, unclean living, and, possibly, treason. On May 30, Marlowe spends the day with four companions, at the tavern of Eleanor Bull, in Deptford. After supper, he quarrels with one of them, Ingram Frizer, and is mortally stabbed through the eye by him. Frizer, successfully claiming self-defense at the inquest, is pardoned on June 18. A few days after Marlowe's death, an

informer, Richard Baines, accuses Marlowe of various blasphemies, treasons, and atheistic opinions. Marlowe is buried at St. Nicholas Church, Deptford.

1594   *Edward II* and *Dido, Queen of Carthage* published.

1598   *Hero and Leander* published. Chapman finishes *Hero and Leander,* and this new version published. Marlowe's version of Ovid's *Elegies* published.

1599   *The Passionate Shepherd to His Love* published.

1600   *Lucans First Booke Translated Line by Line* published.

1601–2   *The Massacre at Paris* published.

1604   A text of *Doctor Faustus* published.

1616   B text of *Doctor Faustus* published.

1633   *The Jew of Malta* published; performed at the Cockpit and the Court.

Contributors

HAROLD BLOOM, Sterling Professor of the Humanities at Yale University, is the author of *The Anxiety of Influence, Poetry and Repression,* and many other volumes of literary criticism. His forthcoming study, *Freud: Transference and Authority,* attempts a full-scale reading of all of Freud's major writings. A MacArthur Prize Fellow, he is general editor of five series of literary criticism published by Chelsea House. During 1987–88, he served as Charles Eliot Norton Professor of Poetry at Harvard University.

G. K. HUNTER is Professor of English at Yale University and Honorary Professor at the University of Warwick. He is the author of *Dramatic Identities and Cultural Tradition,* a collection of essays on Shakespeare, and of studies of Lyly, Webster, Peele, and Milton.

WILBUR SANDERS is the author of *The Dramatist and the Received Idea* and *John Donne's Poetry.*

EDWARD A. SNOW is Professor of English at Rice University and the author of *A Study of Vermeer.*

BARBARA HOWARD TRAISTER is a member of the English Department at Lehigh University. She is the author of *Heavenly Necromancers: The Magician in English Renaissance Drama.*

JOHANNES H. BIRRINGER is Lecturer in English at Yale University and the author of *Marlowe's* Doctor Faustus *and* Tamburlaine: *Theological and Theatrical Perspectives.*

JONATHAN DOLLIMORE is Lecturer in English at the University of Sussex. He is the author of *Radical Tragedy* and the co-editor of *Political Shakespeare: New Essays in Cultural Materialism* and *Selected Plays of John Webster.*

CHRISTOPHER RICKS is Professor of English at Boston University. His books include studies of Milton and Keats. He is the editor of the now standard edition of *The Poems of Tennyson.*

Brooke, Nicholas. "The Moral Tragedy of Doctor Faustus." *Cambridge Journal* 7 (1952): 662–87.

Brooks, Cleanth. "The Unity of Marlowe's *Dr Faustus*." In *To Nevill Coghill from Friends,* edited by J. Lawlor and W. H. Auden. London: Faber & Faber, 1966.

Campbell, Lily B. "*Doctor Faustus:* A Case of Conscience." *PMLA* 67 (1952): 219–39.

Cheney, Patrick. "Love and Magic in *Doctor Faustus:* Marlowe's Indictment of Spenserian Idealism." *Mosaic* 17, no. 4 (1984): 93–109.

Cole, Douglas. *Suffering and Evil in the Plays of Christopher Marlowe.* Princeton: Princeton University Press, 1962.

Cutts, John P. *The Left Hand of God: A Critical Interpretation of the Plays of Christopher Marlowe.* Haddonfield, N.J.: Haddonfield House, 1973.

Danson, Lawrence. "Christopher Marlowe: The Questioner." *English Literary Renaissance* 12 (1982): 3–29.

Davidson, Clifford. "Doctor Faustus of Wittenberg." *Studies in Philology* 59 (1962): 514–23.

Eliot, T. S. *Elizabethan Essays.* London: Faber & Faber, 1934.

Ellis-Fermor, Una M. "Christopher Marlowe." *Michigan Quarterly Review* 12 (1973): 136–59.

Frye, R. M. "Marlowe's *Doctor Faustus:* The Repudiation of Humanity." *The South Atlantic Quarterly* 55 (1956): 322–28.

Gardner, Helen. "Milton's 'Satan' and the Theme of Damnation in Elizabethan Tragedy." *English Studies* 1 (1948): 46–66.

Giamatti, A. Bartlett. "Marlowe: The Arts of Illusion." *Yale Review* 61 (1972): 530–43.

Godshalk, W. L. *The Marlovian World Picture.* The Hague: Mouton, 1974.

Goldberg, Jonathan. "Sodomy and Society: The Case of Christopher Marlowe." *Southwest Review* 69 (1984): 371–90.

Golden, Kenneth L. "Myth, Psychology, and Marlowe's *Doctor Faustus*." *College Literature* 12 (1985): 202–10.

Greenblatt, Stephen. *Renaissance Self-Fashioning: From More to Shakespeare.* Chicago: University of Chicago Press, 1980.

Greg, W. W. "The Damnation of Faustus." *The Modern Language Review* 41 (1946): 97–107.

———, ed. *Marlowe's* Doctor Faustus *1604–1616: Parallel Texts.* Oxford: Clarendon, 1950.

Hattaway, Michael. "The Theology of Marlowe's *Doctor Faustus.*" *Renaissance Drama* 3 (1970): 52–78.

The Historie of the Damnable Life, and Deserved Death of Doctor John Faustus. In *The Sources of the Faust Tradition from Simon Magus to Lessing,* edited by Philip Mason Palmer and Robert Pattison More. 1952. Reprint. New York: Haskell House, 1965.

Homan, Sidney R. "Chapman and Marlowe: The Paradoxical Hero and the Divided Response." *Journal of English and Germanic Philology* 68 (1969): 391–406.

Honderich, Pauline. "John Calvin and Doctor Faustus." *The Modern Language Review* 68 (1973): 1–13.

Jump, John, ed. *Marlowe,* Doctor Faustus: *A Casebook.* London: Macmillan, 1969.

Kernan, Alvin, ed. *Two Renaissance Mythmakers: Christopher Marlowe and Ben Jonson*. Baltimore: Johns Hopkins University Press, 1977.

Kirschbaum, Leo. "Marlowe's *Faustus*: A Reconsideration." *The Review of English Studies* 19 (1943): 225–41.

Knights, L. C. "The Strange Case of Christopher Marlowe." In *Further Explorations*. London: Chatto & Windus, 1965.

Kocher, Paul H. *Christopher Marlowe: A Study of His Thought, Learning and Character.* Chapel Hill: University of North Carolina Press, 1946.

Leech, Clifford, ed. *Marlowe: A Collection of Critical Essays*. Englewood Cliffs, N.J.: Prentice-Hall, 1964.

Levin, Harry. *The Overreacher: A Study of Christopher Marlowe*. Cambridge: Harvard University Press, 1952.

Levin, Richard. *The Multiple Plot in English Renaissance Drama*. Chicago: University of Chicago Press, 1971.

McAlindon, T. *English Renaissance Tragedy*. London: Macmillan, 1986.

Mahood, M. M. "Marlowe's Heroes." In *Poetry and Humanism*. London: Jonathan Cape, 1950.

Manley, Frank. "The Nature of Faustus." *Modern Philology* 66 (1969): 218–31.

Masington, Charles G. *Christopher Marlowe's Tragic Vision: A Study in Damnation*. Athens: Ohio University Press, 1972.

Matalene, H. W. "Marlowe's *Faustus* and the Comforts of Academism." *ELH* 39 (1972): 495–519.

Maxwell, J. C. "The Sin of Faustus." *The Wind and the Rain* 4 (1947): 49–52.

Morris, Brian, ed. *Christopher Marlowe*. London: Mermaid Critical Commentaries, 1968.

O'Brian, Margaret Ann. "Christian Belief in *Doctor Faustus*." *ELH* 37 (1970): 1–10.

Ornstein, Robert. "The Comic Synthesis in *Doctor Faustus*." *ELH* 22 (1955): 165–72.

Palmer, D. J. "Magic and Poetry in *Doctor Faustus*." *Critical Quarterly* 6 (1964): 56–67.

Poirer, Michel. *Christopher Marlowe*. London: Chatto & Windus, 1951.

Powell, Jocelyn. "Marlowe's Spectacle." *The Drama Review* 8, no. 4 (1964): 195–210.

Sachs, Arieh. "The Religious Despair of Doctor Faustus." *Journal of English and Germanic Philology* 63 (1964): 625–47.

Sanders, Wilbur. *The Dramatist and the Received Idea: Studies in the Plays of Marlowe and Shakespeare*. Cambridge: Cambridge University Press, 1968.

Sewall, Richard B. *The Vision of Tragedy*. New Haven: Yale University Press, 1959.

Smith, James. "Marlowe's *Doctor Faustus*." *Scrutiny* 8 (1939–40): 36–55.

Steane, J. B. *Marlowe: A Critical Study*. Cambridge: Cambridge University Press, 1964.

Stroup, Thomas B. "*Doctor Faustus* and *Hamlet*: Contrasting Kinds of Christian Tragedy." *Comparative Drama* 5 (1972): 243–53.

Tomlinson, T. B. *A Study of Elizabethan and Jacobean Tragedy*. Cambridge: Cambridge University Press, 1964.

Waith, Eugene M. *The Herculean Hero in Marlowe, Chapman, Shakespeare, and Dryden*. New York: Columbia University Press, 1962.

Warren, Michael J. "*Doctor Faustus:* The Old Man and the Text." *English Literary Renaissance* 11 (1981): 111–47.

West, Robert H. "The Impatient Magic of Dr. Faustus." *English Literary Renaissance* 4 (1974): 218–40.

Wilson, F. P. *Marlowe and the Early Shakespeare.* Oxford: Clarendon, 1953.

Acknowledgments

"Five-Act Structure in *Doctor Faustus*" by G. K. Hunter from *Dramatic Identities and Cultural Tradition: Studies in Shakespeare and His Contemporaries* by G. K. Hunter, © 1978 by G. K. Hunter. Reprinted by permission of the author, Barnes & Noble Books, Totowa, New Jersey, and Liverpool University Press. This essay originally appeared in *Tulane Drama Review* 8, no. 4 (1964), © 1964 by *Tulane Drama Review.* Reprinted by permission of the MIT Press, Cambridge, Massachusetts.

"Doctor Faustus's Sin" (originally entitled "The New Wine and the Old Bottles: 'Doctor Faustus'") by Wilbur Sanders from *The Dramatist and the Received Idea: Studies in the Plays of Marlowe & Shakespeare* by Wilbur Sanders, © 1968 by Cambridge University Press. Reprinted by permission.

"Marlowe's *Doctor Faustus* and the Ends of Desire" by Edward A. Snow from *Two Renaissance Mythmakers: Christopher Marlowe and Ben Jonson,* edited by Alvin Kernan, © 1977 by the English Institute. Reprinted by permission of the Johns Hopkins University Press, Baltimore/London.

"*Doctor Faustus*: Master of Self-Delusion" by Barbara Howard Traister from *Heavenly Necromancers: The Magician in English Renaissance Drama* by Barbara Howard Traister, © 1984 by the Curators of the University of Missouri. Reprinted by permission of the University of Missouri Press.

"Faustus's Rhetoric of Aspiration" by Johannes H. Birringer from *Marlowe's Dr Faustus and Tamburlaine: Theological and Theatrical Perspectives* by Johannes H. Birringer, © 1984 by Verlag Peter Lang GmbH, Frankfurt am Main. Reprinted by permission.

"*Doctor Faustus* (ca. 1589–92): Subversion through Transgression" by Jonathan Dollimore from *Radical Tragedy: Religion, Ideology and Power in the Drama of Shakespeare and His Contemporaries* by Jonathan Dollimore, © 1984 by Jonathan Dollimore. Reprinted by permission of the University of Chicago Press and the Harvester Press Ltd.

"*Doctor Faustus* and Hell on Earth" by Christopher Ricks from *Essays in Criticism* 35, no. 2 (April 1985), © 1985 by Christopher Ricks. Reprinted by permission.

141

Index

143